DIGITAL DIPLOMA MILLS
The Automation of Higher Education

Publication of this book was assisted by a contribution from
THE JUDY RUBEN OUTREACH FUND

DIGITAL DIPLOMA MILLS
The Automation of Higher Education

David F. Noble

Monthly Review Press
New York

Library of Congress Cataloging-in-Publication Data
Noble, David F.
    Digital diploma mills : the automation of higher education / by David F. Noble.
        p.cm.
    Includes bibliographical references and index.
    ISBN 1-58367-061-0 (cloth) ISBN 1-58367-092-0 (pbk)
    1. Education, Higher–Effect of technological innovations on–United States
    –History.
    2. Universities and colleges–Technological innovations–United States–History.
    I. Title.

    LB2395.7 .N63 2001
    378'.00285–dc21   2001057931

Monthly Review Press
127 West 27st Street
New York, NY 10001

Design and production by Terry J. Allen, New York, NY

Manufactured in Canada
10 9 8 7 6 5 4 3 2

Contents

In memory of Stan Weir

"We may quail before the course of history as before a relentlessly riding tidal wave, and we may be swept along. But we join in building dikes, and men have been able to stand fast. History differs from the tides of the sea. Those tides are mute. History speaks, and we answer."

— *Karl Jaspers*

Preface to the Paperback Edition

Online education? The notion already sounds a bit dated. Just a moment ago heralded as the future of education, it has already become history. And as we slowly regain our composure in the aftermath of the dot-com hysteria that swept through academia, we must ask ourselves, in retrospect, what was that? and answer, a scam of monumental proportions. The premature demise of this seeming juggernaut confirms the central thesis of this book, that the campus craze for computer-based instruction was never really about education at all, but about making money, and the opportunities and careers that went with it. And now that the money is gone, now that the sober economic realities of online education have set in, now that the speculators have soured on the education market and the venture capitalists and entrepreneurs have moved on to greener pastures, the enterprise has collapsed, leaving campuses across the continent strewn with the debris of the fast-talking flim-flam artists of academia.

The bubble has burst (as I early anticipated in Chapter Four of this book), but the damage remains. The sad truth is that this episode of excess has left behind a legacy that will burden higher education for years to come. A physical infrastructure representing hundreds of millions of dollars of mostly taxpayer investment will need to be maintained, upgraded, and "supported," at the continued expense of quality education—a technological tapeworm in the guts of higher education feeding off its host. Meanwhile a plethora of half-baked but costly projects hatched during the hysteria still clog the pipelines, awaiting the light of day, while others are just now making their belated appearance, dead on arrival, to take up space and suck up scarce resources.

At the same time, a cadre of opportunists and careerists who rode the wave to positions of prominence and power remain entrenched, at or near the top of the hierarchy, despite their contribution to the calamity. "The truth is that the e-learning technology itself, and those of us who represent the institutional and corporate agents of change in the e-learning environment, have thus far failed," Lev Gonick, vice president and Chief Information Officer at Case Western Reserve University, acknowledged to the *New York Times* (May

4, 2002). But Gonick neglected to note that, despite the failure of the enterprise he championed, he himself succeeded handsomely, metamorphosing in the process from an obscure scholar to one of the chief officials of a major institution. And this is just one of many such successes generated by failure. We can be guaranteed, moreover, that these people will never be held accountable for damages by the very institutions they now run. Rather they will work in myriad, albeit more subtle, ways to keep their game going, changing their vocabulary, enlisting innocent but ambitious recruits, inventing a stream of harebrained schemes to secure their positions and enlarge their empires. The costs to students and faculty, to learning and teaching, to the invaluable ennobling missions of the university, need not concern them. For they now know, more than ever before, that, in academia at least, they can get away with almost anything.

Toronto, November 2002

Introduction

This book began life as a series of articles on the automation of higher education, written from the trenches. Having studied the automation of other industries and its consequences for the workers of those industries, especially in my book *Forces of Production*, and having tried in my own way to contribute to their struggles, I suddenly and unexpectedly became witness to the very same assault on the industry in which I worked. What I had learned, what I presumed to know, would now be put to the test of practice, on my colleagues' and my own behalf. Did historical understanding and experience of the trials of others give us any advantage in our own? What were the lessons of those earlier episodes that might be applied here, to forestall and potentially reverse this latest offensive on people's lives and livelihoods?

First and foremost, my knowledge endowed me with a small degree of foresight, and the conviction that all too often in the past people had only belatedly realized the dimensions of the calamity that had befallen them, too late to act effectively in their own interest. Thus, above all these articles were written to sound an early alarm, a warning timely enough to provide some opportunity for defensive preparation and the envisioning of alternatives.

Second, as a scholar, journalist, and activist I have chronicled and fought against the commercialization and corporatization of higher education. In my first book, *America by Design*, I described the distant origins of this development during the first three decades of the twentieth century. At around the same time, in the mid-1970s, I began to observe a contemporary recapitulation of this earlier episode and, as a journalist, reported on the increasing collaboration between academia and corporate industry, particularly in the area of scientific and technological research. (The earliest of these articles is included as an Appendix to this volume.)

At the same time, as an activist, I undertook efforts with others to alert people both within and without academia to the threat to the integrity of academic research that such collaboration entailed. These efforts culminated in the establishment of the National Coalition for Universities in the Public Interest, which I founded in 1983 with Ralph Nader and Al Meyerhoff. This organization, under the direction of Leonard Minsky, concentrated on the media, the courts, and congressional hearings to bring extra-academic pressure to bear upon university administrations who were selling out their colleagues and the public in the pursuit of corporate partnerships. As well, the organization sought to galvanize student and faculty opposition to the corporatization if their institutions, chronicling the consequences of this trend while aiding those who suffered abuse and retribution for refusing to go along. In most of these efforts, attention was focused on the commercialization of academic research, and the related neglect of the educational function of universities at the expense, both literally and figuratively, of students. In the mid-1990s, this situation began to change with the belated commodification and commercialization of this educational function by means of online delivery. Like research, the instructional activity of the academy had now come to be viewed by academic administrators and their corporate partners as a "profit center." *Digital Diploma Mills* describes in detail this extension of academic commerce from research into instruction, the heart and soul of academia.

Third, as a student of the social history of technology who had devoted thirty years of scholarship to disclosing the political, economic, and cultural underside, and ideological origins, of so-called technological progress, I observed with dismay how technology was once again being used as a vehicle of, and cover for, political agendas, this time within academia itself. Hence, as I had done in other arenas, I undertook to examine the political economy of online education. The results of this undertaking now fill these pages. At the same time, I sought to expose the ideological compulsions, rooted in a blind faith in the necessity and ultimate beneficence of technological innovation that both propels proponents of this seemingly "technology-driven" institutional transformation and handicaps the opposition.

In earlier books, *Progress Without People* and *The Religion of Technology*, I had described the nature, sources, and effects of this peculiar yet hegemonic system of belief that was now contributing to the mindless deformation, degradation, and delimitation of institutions presumably dedicated to the life of the mind. Caught up in, or paralyzed by, this ubiquitous enchantment, faculty for the most part confronted this fundamental threat to the integrity of academia not with the creative and critical thought and robust and rigorous debate supposedly emblematic of academia but rather with the same fear, defensiveness, fatalism, and silence characteristic of all other hapless victims of seemingly technologically driven assault. Their disarray is understandable for their fear is warranted. The ideology of technological progress takes no prisoners. In this cultural context, any and all critics are at once disarmed and marginalized, dismissed as ignorant cranks, Luddites, and lunatics who dare to stand in the way of inevitable progress. Their criticism, however compelling in evidence and argument, is not taken seriously because it is beyond the bounds of respectable discourse, irrelevant and irreverent, heresy. Little wonder, then, that in this environment thoughtful people tend to keep their wayward thoughts to themselves.

And for those of us for whom silence in the face of injustice, even that clothed in the garb of technological progress, is not an option, there is a price to pay. My own continuously careening academic career testifies to that fact, having been fired from jobs at MIT and the Smithsonian Institution, two citadels of the faith, for my critiques of technological progress. When the students at Harvey Mudd College, an elite engineering school where I recently taught for two years, voted to have me as their commencement speaker, despite my having been defamed by the administration as "anti-technology" (whatever that means), the president blocked it. When I successfully opposed the establishment of the International Space University, a finishing school for space cadets, at my current institution, York University, I was publicly assailed by my own president as "anti-science" and even "anti-intellectual." Even as I write this, my appointment to the endowed Woodsworth Professorship in the Humanities at Simon Fraser University is being blocked by equally ideologically blinded administrators because of my criticism of online education and the corporatization of academia.

Moreover, and perhaps most disconcerting of all, is the fact that even otherwise insightful people are captive to the same ideology, as the peculiar publication history of the original articles attests. The first article in the series—now Chapter Two of this volume—was originally commissioned by Katrina Vanden Heuvel, editor of *The Nation*. When it was delivered, however, she and her staff refused to publish it, declining even to consider any revision. Likewise, the editor of *Lingua Franca* rejected the piece outright. It seems that these people too, however critical in other respects, are constrained, when it comes to any discussion of technology, by the same boundaries of respectable discourse that inhibit those who run the universities and their quiescent would-be opponents. They apparently feared being tarred, by association, by the same ideological brush that has tarnished my academic reputation and undone other critics of technological progress. Happily, the article was ultimately published on the Internet, through which it was enthusiastically received as a "manifesto" of resistance, distributed worldwide, and repeatedly republished, as were the subsequent articles in the series.

There are some who would see an irony, indeed a contradiction, in this, that the author of a critique of computer-based education would use the Internet as a medium of publication, that a critic of technology would use technology to his advantage. But such a perception merely reflects the Manichean worldview of the ideology of technological progress which, like other dogmatic belief systems, allows for only orthodoxy or heresy, in this case "pro-technology" or "anti-technology" (sometimes psychologized as "techno-phobia"). But it is precisely the mind-numbing effect of such meaningless and dangerous categories that has been the focus of nearly all of my work. A critic of technological development is no more "anti-technology" than a movie critic is "anti-movie." Would anyone see it as ironic, or contradictory, to find that movie critics go to the movies? Or dance critics to dance performances, or art critics to galleries and museums? The aim of criticism is not indiscriminate rejection but rather sober, serious, and sustained scrutiny and evaluation as the basis for informed and enlightened discrimination. The point is neither to embrace nor to reject technology but to use it wisely.

Finally, as a working-class, first-generation beneficiary of public higher education, a graduate of the University of Florida, I have a deep and abiding appreciation for what is at stake here in the struggle over the future of academia. I left Miami for the university ignorant, unaware of my world and of my place in it. There I met kinds of people I never knew existed, people who dedicated their lives to ideas, to understanding the world, to transmitting and thinking critically and imaginatively about the received wisdom of our culture. The experience changed my life as it has changed the lives of countless others. In the not too distant future, young people with a background like mine—that is, without means—will not be welcomed to the campus and into the community of this rare kind of people for a genuine education, but will be told instead to go online for training, and to do it all alone. It goes without saying that it is not the same, that something essential will have been lost, but in time that will be all that anyone remembers. The struggle ahead is to forestall that dismal future. If it is about job security and academic freedom and scholarly integrity and the public's trust in its institutional heritage, it is, above all, about the preservation and extension of affordable, accessible, quality education for everyone who wants it. In the end, that is what this book is about, not technology, not even power, but the perpetuation of promise.

Toronto, 2001

1

Lessons from a Pre-Digital Age:
The Correspondence Education Movement

"Those who cannot remember the past are condemned to repeat it."
— *George Santayana*

All discussion of distance education these days invariably turns into a discussion of technology, an endless meditation on the wonders of computer-mediated instruction. Identified with a revolution in technology, distance education has thereby assumed the aura of innovation and the appearance of a revolution itself, a bold departure from tradition, a signal step toward a preordained and radically transformed higher educational future. In the face of such a seemingly inexorable technology-driven destiny and the seductive enchantment of technological transcendence, skeptics are silenced and all questions are begged. But we pay a price for this technological fetishism that so dominates and delimits discussion. For it prevents us from perceiving the more fundamental significance of today's drive for distance education, which, at bottom, is not really about technology, nor is it anything new. We have been here before.

In essence, the current mania for distance education is about the commodification of higher education, of which computer technology is merely the latest medium, and it is, in reality, more a rerun than a revolution, bearing striking resemblance to a past today's enthusiasts barely know about or care to acknowledge, an earlier episode in the commodification of higher education known as correspondence instruction or, more quaintly, home study. Then as now, distance education has always been not so much technology-driven as profit-driven, whatever the mode of delivery. The common denominator linking the two episodes is not technology but the pursuit of profit in the guise and name of higher education. A careful examination of the earlier, pre-computer, episode in distance education enables us to place the current mania not only in historical perspective but also in its proper political-economic context. The chief aim here is to try to shift our attention from technology to political economy, and from fantasies about the future to the far more sobering lessons of the past.

Before proceeding with the historical analysis, it is important to spell out what is meant by both education and commodification, since these terms are often used with little precision. To begin with, education must be distinguished from training (which is arguably more suitable for distance delivery), because the two are so often conflated. In essence, training involves the honing of a person's mind so that his or her mind can be used for the purposes of someone other than that person. Training thus typically entails a radical divorce between knowledge and the self. Here knowledge is usually defined as a set of skills or a body of information designed to be put to use, to become operational, only in a context determined by someone other than the trained person; in this context the assertion of self is not only counterproductive, it is subversive to the enterprise. Education is the exact opposite of training in that it entails not the disassociation but the utter integration of knowledge and the self, in a word, self-knowledge. Here knowledge is defined by and, in turn, helps to define, the self. Knowledge and the knowledgeable person are basically inseparable.

Education is a process that necessarily entails an interpersonal (not merely interactive) relationship between people—student and teacher (and student and student) that aims at individual and collective self-knowledge. (Whenever people recall their educational experiences they tend to remember above all not courses or subjects or the information imparted but people, people who changed their minds or their lives, people who made a difference in their developing sense of themselves. It is a sign of our current confusion about education that we must be reminded of this obvious fact: that the relationship between people is central to the educational experience.) Education is a process of becoming for all parties, based upon mutual recognition and validation and centering upon the formation and evolution of identity. The actual content of the educational experience is defined by this relationship between people and the chief determinant of quality education is the establishment and enrichment of this relationship.

Like education, the word commodification (or commoditization) is used rather loosely with regard to education and some precision might help the discussion. A commodity is something created, grown, produced, or manufactured for exchange on the market. There are, of course, some things that are bought and sold on the market that were not created for that purpose, such as "labor"and land—what the political economist Karl Polanyi referred to as "fictitious commodities." Most educational offerings, although divided into units of credit and exchanged for tuition, are fictitious commodities in that they are not created by the educator strictly with this purpose in mind. Here we will be using the term commodity, not in this fictitious, more expansive, sense but rather in its classical, restricted sense, to mean something expressly created for market exchange. The commodification of higher education, then, refers to the deliberate transformation of the educational process into commodity form, for the purpose of commercial transaction.

The commodification of education requires the interruption of this fundamental educational process and the disintegration and distillation of the educational experience into discrete, reified, and ultimately saleable things or packages of things. In the first step toward commodification, attention is shifted from the experience of the people involved in the educational process to the production and inventorying of an assortment of fragmented "course materials": syllabi, lectures, lessons, exams (now referred to in the aggregate as "content"). As anyone familiar with higher education knows, these common instruments of instruction barely reflect what actually takes place in the educational experience, and lend an illusion of order and predictability to what is, at its best, an essentially unscripted and undetermined process. Second, these fragments are removed or "alienated" from their original context, the actual educational process itself, and from their producers, the teachers, and are assembled as "courses," which take on an existence independent of and apart from those who created and gave flesh to them. This is perhaps the most critical step in commodity formation. The alienation of ownership of and control over course material (through surrender of copyright) is crucial to this step. Finally, the assembled "courses" are exchanged for a profit on the market, which determines their value, by their "owners," who may or may not have any relationship to the original creators and participants in the educational process. At the expense of the original integrity of the educational process, instruction has here been transformed into a set of deliverable commodities, and the end of education has become not self-knowledge but the making of money. In the wake of this transformation, teachers become commodity producers and deliverers, subject to the familiar regime of commodity production in any other industry, and students become consumers of yet more commodities. The relationship between teacher and student is thus reestablished, in an alienated mode, through the medium of the market, and the buying and selling of commodities takes on the appearance of education. But it is, in reality, only a shadow of education, an assemblage of pieces without the whole.

Again, under this new regime, painfully familiar to skilled workers in every industry since the dawn of industrial capitalism, educators confront the harsh realities of commodity production: speedup, routinization of work, greater work discipline and managerial supervision, reduced autonomy, job insecurity, employer appropriation of the fruits of their labor, and, above all, the insistent managerial pressures to reduce labor costs in order to turn a profit. Thus, the commoditization of instruction leads invariably to the "proletarianization" or, more politely, the "deprofessionalization" of the professoriate. (As investors shift their focus from health care to education, the deprofessionalization experienced by physicians is being extended to professors, who now face what some Wall Street spokesmen are already calling EMOs, the education counterpart to HMOs.)

But there is a paradox at the core of this transformation. Quality education is labor-intensive, it depends upon a low teacher-student ratio, and significant interaction between the two parties—the one utterly unambiguous result of a century of educational research. Any effort to offer quality in education must therefore presuppose a substantial and sustained investment in educational labor, whatever the medium of instruction. The requirements of commodity production, however, undermine the labor-intensive foundation of quality education (and with it, quality products people will willingly pay for). Pedagogical promise and economic efficiency are thus in contradiction. Here is the Achilles' heel of distance education. In the past as well as the present, distance educators have always insisted that they offer a kind of intimate and individualized instruction not possible in the crowded, competitive environment of the campus. Theirs is an improved, enhanced education. To make their enterprise profitable, however, they have been compelled to reduce their instructional costs to a minimum, thereby undermining their pedagogical promise. The invariable result has been not only a degraded labor force but a degraded product as well. Thus, what is at stake in the struggle over the commodification of education is not only the professional autonomy and working conditions of educators but our understanding of education itself. The history of correspondence education provides a cautionary tale in this regard, a lesson of a debacle hardly heeded by those today so frantically engaged in repeating it.

The rhetoric of the correspondence education movement a century ago was almost identical to that of the current distance education movement: anytime, anywhere education (they didn't yet use the word "asynchronous"), accessible to anyone from home or workplace, advance at your own pace, profit from personalized, one-on-one contact with your instructor, avoiding the crowded classroom and boring lecture hall. In brief, correspondence instruction emerged in the last decade of the nineteenth century along two parallel paths, as a commercial, for-profit enterprise, and as an extension of university-based higher education. At the heart of both was the production and distribution of prepackaged courses of instruction, educational commodities bought, sold, and serviced through the mail.

The commercial effort arose in the expectation of profiting from the growing demand for vocational and professional training, generated by increasingly mechanized and science-based industrial activity, and rapidly devolved into what became known as diploma mills. The university effort arose in response to the same demand for vocational training, as an attempt to protect traditional academic turf from commercial competition, to tap into a potent new source of revenues, and as a result of a genuinely progressive movement for democratic access to education, particularly adult education. While the universities tried initially to distinguish themselves in both form and content from their increasingly disreputable commercial rivals, in the end, having embarked down the same path of commodity production, they tended invariably to resemble them, becoming diploma mills in their own right.

The parallels with the present situation are striking. For-profit commercial firms are once again emerging to provide vocational training to working people via computer-based distance instruction. Universities are once again striving to meet the challenge of these commercial enterprises, generate new revenue streams, and extend the range and reach of their offerings. And although trying somehow to distinguish themselves from their commercial rivals—while collaborating ever more closely with them—they are once again coming to resemble them, this time as digital diploma mills. In the following pages we will examine in some detail the history of the correspondence education movement in the United States, looking first at the commercial ventures and then at the parallel efforts of the universities. The account of the university experience is based upon heretofore unexamined archival records of four of the leading institutions engaged in correspondence instruction: the University of Chicago, Columbia University, the University of Wisconsin, and the University of California, Berkeley. Although based upon different technologies from the online university—the railroad and the postal service rather than computers and fiber-optic cable—the correspondence education movement exemplified the same logic of commodification.

Thomas J. Foster established one of the earliest private, for-profit correspondence schools in Pennsylvania in the late 1880s to provide vocational training in mining, mine safety, drafting and metalworking. Spurred by the success of these efforts, he founded in 1892 the International Correspondence Schools, which became one of the largest and most enduring enterprises in this burgeoning new education industry. By 1926 there were over three hundred such schools in the United States, with an annual income of over $70 million (one and a half times the income of all colleges and universities combined), with fifty new schools being started each year. In 1924 these commercial enterprises, which catered primarily to people who sought qualifications for job advancement in business and industry, boasted of an enrollment four times that of all colleges, universities, and professional schools combined. Copyrighted courses were developed for the firms in-house by their own staff or under contract with outside "experts," and were administered through the mail by in-house or contract instructors. Students were recruited through advertisements and myriad promotional schemes, peddled by a field sales force employed on a commission basis.

In their promotional activities and material, targeted to credulous and inexperienced youth, the commercial firms claimed that their courses would guarantee students careers, security, wealth, status, and self-respect. "If you want to be independent," one firm pitched, "if you want to make good in the world; if you want to get off somebody's payroll and head one of your own; if you want the many pleasures and luxuries that are in the world for you and your family; if you want to banish forever the fear of losing your job, then, sign the pay-raising enrollment blank! Get it to me! Right now!" The chief selling point of education by means of correspondence, the firms maintained, was personalized instruction for busy people. "The student has the individual attention of the teacher while he is reciting, though it is in writing," another firm explained. The student "works at his own tempo set by himself and not fixed by the average capacities of a large number of students studying simultaneously. He can begin when he likes, study at any hours convenient to him, and finish as soon as he is able."

In all of the firms a priority was placed upon securing enrollment and the lion's share of effort and revenues was expended in promotion and sales rather than in instruction. Typically between 50 and 80 percent of tuition fees went into direct mail campaigns, magazine and newspaper advertisements, and the training and support of a sales staff responsible for "cold canvassing," soliciting "prospects" and intensive follow-ups and paid by the number of enrollments they obtained. "The most intensive work of all the schools is, in fact, devoted to developing the sales force," John Noffsinger observed in his 1926 Carnegie Corporation–sponsored study of correspondence schools written when the correspondence movement was at its peak. "This is by far the most highly organized and carefully worked out department of the school." "The whole emphasis on salesmanship is the most serious criticism to be made against the system of correspondence education as it now exists," Noffsinger noted. "Perhaps it cannot be avoided when schools are organized for profit," he added.

Indeed, the pursuit of profit tended inescapably to subvert the noble intentions, or pretensions, of the enterprises, especially in what had become a highly competitive (and totally unregulated) field in which many firms came and went and some made handsome fortunes. In a burgeoning industry increasingly dominated by hucksters and swindlers who had little genuine knowledge of or interest in education per se, promotional claims were easily exaggerated to the point of fraud and the sales forces were encouraged to sign up any and all prospects, however ill-prepared for the coursework, in order to fulfill their quotas and reap their commissions (which often amounted to as much as a third of the tuition). Enrollees were typically required to pay the full tuition or a substantial part of it up front and most of the firms had a no-refund policy for the 90 to 95 percent of the students who failed to complete their course of study. (In Noffsinger's survey of seventy-five correspondence schools only 2.6 percent of the enrolled students completed the courses they had begun.)

The remarkably high dropout rate was not an accident. It reflected not only the shameless methods of recruitment but also the shoddy quality of what was being offered—the inevitable result of the profit-driven commodification of education. If the lion's share of revenues were expended on promotion—to recruit students and secure the up-front tuition payments—a mere pittance was expended on instruction. In the commercial firms the promotional staff was four to six times—and oftentimes twenty to thirty times—the size of the instructional staff and compensation of the former was typically many times that of the latter. In some firms, less than one cent of every tuition dollar went into instruction. For the actual "delivery" of courses—the correction of lessons and grading exams—most firms relied upon a casualized workforce of "readers" who worked part-time and were paid on a piecework basis per lesson or exam (roughly twenty cents per lesson in the 1920s). Many firms preferred "sub-professional" personnel, particularly untrained older women, for routine grading. These people often worked under sweatshop conditions, having to deliver a high volume of lessons in order to make a living, and were unable therefore to manage more than a perfunctory pedagogical performance. Such conditions were of course not conducive to the kind of careful, individualized instruction promised in the company's promotional materials. (As Noffsinger pointed out in his Carnegie study, "the lack of personal contact between teacher and student" was the "chief weakness" of the instruction.) The central "pedagogical" concern of the firms was clearly to keep instructional costs to a bare minimum, a fact caricatured in vaudeville sketches of correspondence education in which all work was done by a lone mail clerk and the instructors dropped out of sight altogether.

All of this made perfect economic sense, however, and was summed up in correspondence industry jargon in the phrase "dropout money." Since students were required to pay their tuition upfront without the possibility of a refund, and instructors were paid on a piecework basis, once students dropped out there was no further instructional expense and what remained of the up-front payment was pure profit: "dropout money." Given the economics of this cynical education system, there was no incentive whatsoever to try to retain students by upgrading the conditions of instruction and thereby improving the quality of course offerings. The economics in fact dictated the opposite, to concentrate all efforts upon recruitment and next to nothing on instruction. Already by the mid-1920s—when the correspondence movement was at its peak—increasing criticism of the commercial correspondence firms had largely discredited the industry, which was coming to be seen as a haven for disreputable hustlers and diploma mills. In 1924 the New York Board of Regents condemned the schools for their false claims and for their no-refund policies. "There is nothing inherent in correspondence as a method of instruction to disqualify it as a way to education," wrote Noffsinger, an avid supporter of adult distance education (and later official of the National Home Study Council, established to try to regulate the industry). "Unfortunately," however, he lamented, "the majority of correspondence schools are not well equipped and still less conscientiously conducted. They are commercial enterprises designed to make quick and easy profits. Many of them are in the shady zone bordering on the criminal. A large proportion of those who enroll in correspondence courses are wasting time, money, and energy or even are being swindled." Noffsinger condemned "the victimization of hundreds of thousands who now are virtually robbed of savings and whose enthusiasm for education is crushed." In the commercial schools, Noffsinger warned, "the making of profit is their first consideration, a dangerous situation at best in education."

The evolution of university-based correspondence instruction closely paralleled that of the commercial schools. Following some early stillborn experiments in academic correspondence instruction in the 1880s, the university-based movement began in earnest in the 1890s; by the teens and twenties of this century it had become a craze comparable to today's mania for online distance education. The first entrant into the field was the newly founded University of Chicago whose first president, William Rainey Harper, was an early enthusiast for distance education. By the time he moved to Chicago from Yale, Harper had already had considerable experience in teaching via correspondence through the Chautauqua organization in New York State, and he made the Home Study Department one of the founding pillars of the new university. Following the lead of Chicago other institutions soon joined the ranks of the movement, notably the state universities of Wisconsin, Nebraska, Minnesota, Kansas, Oregon, Texas, Missouri, Colorado, Pennsylvania, Indiana, and California. By 1919, when Columbia University launched its home study program, there were already seventy-three colleges and universities offering instruction by correspondence. Emphasizing the democratization of education and hoping to tap into the lucrative market exploited by their commercial rivals, the universities echoed the sales pitch of the private schools.

Hervey F. Mallory, head of the University of Chicago Home Study Department, proclaimed the virtues of individualized instruction, insisting that education by correspondence was akin to a "tutorial relationship" that "may prove to be superior to the usual method of teaching." "The student acts independently and for himself but at the same time, being in contact with the teacher, he is also enabled to secure special help for every difficulty." Correspondence study, the department advertised, offered three "unique advantages": "you receive individual personal attention; you work as rapidly as you can, or as slowly as necessary, unhampered by others as in a regular class"; and your studies "may begin at any time and may be carried on according to any personal schedule and in any place where postal service is available." Mallory insisted that correspondence study offered an education better than anything possible in "the crowded classroom of the ordinary American University." "It is impossible in such a context to treat students as individuals, overcome peer pressure for conformity, encourage students who are shy, slow, intimidated by a class setting." Home study, by contrast, "takes into account individual differences in learning" and the students "may do course work at any time and any place, and at their own personal pace." From the evangelical perspective of its proponents, then, correspondence education was more than just an extension of traditional education; it was an improvement, a means of instruction at once less costly and of higher quality, an advance, in short, which signaled a revolution in higher education. "What warrant is there for believing that the virility of the more ancient type of cloistered college and university could be maintained, except here and there, in our business civilization?" Mallory asked rhetorically. "The day is coming," President Harper prophesied, heralding that revolution, "when the work done by correspondence will be greater in amount than that done in the classroom of our academies and colleges, when the students who shall recite by correspondence will far outnumber those who make oral presentations."

As was the case with the commercial schools here too the promises and expectations of enthusiasts were thwarted by the realities of commodity production. Although they were not for-profit organizations per se, the correspondence programs of the universities were nevertheless largely self-supporting and hence, de facto, profit-oriented; a correspondence program's expenses had to be covered "by profits from its own operations," as Carl Huth of the University of Chicago's Home Study Department put it. And while it was initially assumed that this new form of instruction would be more economically efficient than traditional classroom-based instruction, the pioneers quickly discovered that correspondence instruction was far more costly to operate than they had imagined, owing primarily to the overhead entailed in administration. Almost from the outset, therefore, they found themselves caught up in much the same game as their commercial rivals:

devising promotional schemes to boost enrollment in order to offset growing administrative costs, reducing their course preparation and revision
expenses by standardizing their inventory and relying on "canned courses,"
and, above all, keeping instructional compensation to a minimum through
the use of casual employment and payment by piece rate. Before too long,
with a degraded product and dropout rates almost comparable to that of the
commercial firms, they too had come to depend for their survival upon
"dropout money."

From the outset, the leaders of the university programs pointedly distinguished their work from that of their disreputable commercial counterparts.
It was unfortunate that the universities had "stepped aside to leave large part
of the field of adult education to commercial schools or even to confidence
men and swindlers," Mallory noted, but the new university programs would
correct for that failure. "The most important fact about the university system
of correspondence instruction in contrast to that of the commercial schools,"
he argued, "is the fact of institutional background, and that background is a
great public-service institution—a modern university . . . an organic whole
whose spiritual or immaterial aspects are far more important than the concrete parts." The Home Study Department of the University of Chicago, he
insisted, was "interwoven with the university" and thus reflected its exalted
traditions and mission—what would today be called "brandworthiness."
Accordingly, the Home Study Department initially emphasized that its courses would be taught by the same professors who taught courses on campus
and, indeed, at the outset even President Harper himself offered a course by
correspondence. But within a few years, most of the course delivery was being
handled by an assortment of instructors, readers, associate readers, fellows,
lecturers, associate lecturers, and assistants, their pay meager and their status
low. They were paid on a piece rate basis—roughly thirty cents per lesson and,
under university statutes, received no benefits. Representatives from the regular faculty ranks were largely those at the lower rungs who took on correspondence work in order to supplement their own quite modest salaries. In
order to make out, the Home Study instructors were compelled to take on a
large volume of work that quickly devolved into uninspired drudgery, and it
was understood that there was no future in it.

Initially, the Home Study Program was selective in its recruitment, requiring evidence of a prospective student's ability as a prerequisite for enrolling. A
student had to have sufficient reason for not enrolling as a resident student and

had to "give satisfactory evidence, by examination or otherwise, that he is able to do the work required." (The University of Chicago required at least partial resident matriculation for those seeking degrees and required examinations for credit given by correspondence.) Eventually, however, such entrance requirements were dropped in order to increase enrollments. According to the Home Study brochure some years later, "You need not take an entrance examination, nor present a transcript of work done elsewhere. Your desire to enroll in a particular course will be taken as evidence that you are prepared to do the work of that course." Although there were some early efforts at advertising and salesmanship, these were kept within what were considered proper bounds for a respectable institution of higher education—a university policy lamented by the Home Study Department, especially in the face of competition from other, more aggressive, institutions such as Columbia.

As in the case of the commercial schools here too the reduced quality of the courses combined with the lack of preparation of those enrolled produced a very high dropout rate. And like the commercial schools, the University of Chicago adopted a no-refund policy; tuition was to be paid in full at the time of registration and, once registration was completed, fees were not refundable. As late as 1939, and despite the criticism of commercial schools on just this count, the university's president, Robert Hutchins, the renowned champion of classical education, reaffirmed this policy. "The registration and tuition fee will not be refunded to a student whose application has been accepted and who has been duly enrolled in a course," Hutchins wrote to a correspondence student. "This statement reflects standard practice in correspondence schools everywhere."

Columbia University did not join the correspondence movement until 1919 but quickly became a leader in the field with revenues matched only by the University of Chicago. It owed its success to an unusually ambitious program aimed at a national and international market and an aggressive promotional effort that rivaled that of the commercial schools. A home study program was first proposed in 1915 by James Egbert, Columbia's head of extension, and the idea was enthusiastically endorsed by Columbia's president, Nicholas Murray Butler, an avid supporter of adult education who had earlier in his career been the founding director of Columbia's summer session for part-time students. In full flower by the mid-twenties, the Columbia correspondence program was providing instruction to students in every state and fifty foreign countries.

Although Columbia never gave academic credit for its correspondence courses aside from a certificate of completion, the university nevertheless strove to distinguish its offerings from those of the commercial schools, emphasizing "personal contact and supervision," concentrating on recognized academic subjects, limiting the number of students in each course, and keeping standards high through regular review of material by the appropriate academic faculty. The twofold aim of home study, according to Egbert, was to extend the enlightening reach of the university while at the same time generating additional revenue. He and his colleagues soon discovered, however, that the preparation of course materials and the administration of the program were more demanding, labor-intensive, and expensive than had been anticipated. To offset these costs, they moved to broaden the correspondence curriculum into more lucrative vocational areas of every sort and to expand their promotional activities in an effort to enlarge the enrollment. In 1920 home study had 156 students; by 1926 there were nearly five thousand and that number was doubled by 1929. As Egbert undertook "to apply business methods" to his expanding operation, the program employed a national sales force of sixty "field representatives" (as compared to one hundred instructors) who were paid a commission according to the number of students they enrolled.

In addition, Columbia mounted a full-scale national advertising campaign in the manner of the commercial firms, with such themes as "Profit by Your Capacity to Learn," "Will You Increase Your Fixed Assets?," "Turning Leisure to Profit," "Who Controls Your Future?", "Who Is Too Old to Learn?" and "Of What Can You Be Certain?" In 1929 Egbert proudly unveiled plans for a vastly expanded enterprise that would be housed in a new twelve-story building. Compared to the lavish expenditure on promotion, the home study program kept its instructional expenses to a minimum. Here too all payment for instruction was on a piece rate, per lesson basis. As at Chicago, while some faculty engaged in home study in order to supplement their salaries, they were likely to be "academic lame ducks," as one home study official described them, and the bulk of instruction was performed by a casualized low-status workforce of instructors, lecturers, and assistants. Overworked and undervalued, they were not quite able or inclined to provide the "personal contact" that was promised. While the Home Study Department continued to boast that all of their courses were "prepared so as to enable the instructor to adjust all study to the individual needs of each student," that "direct contact is maintained between the student and the instructor *personally* [emphasis in original] throughout the course," and that correspondence students "can attain the many advantages of instruction of University grade, under the constant guidance, suggestion, and help of regular members of the University teaching staff," the reality was otherwise. Together with fraudulent advertising and an indiscriminate enrollment policy, inescapably perfunctory instruction produced a dropout rate of 80 percent, a rate comparable to that of the for-profit commercial schools.

The experience of two of the largest state university correspondence programs, Wisconsin and California (Berkeley), was similar to that of the private Chicago and Columbia, even though their institutions could draw upon public funds, because here too the departments were required to be largely self-supporting (public subsidy might be available for overhead but not instruction, which had to be borne by student fees). The Regents authorized correspondence courses at Wisconsin as early as 1891, a year before the University of Chicago, but it was not until 1906 that an actual correspondence department was established as part of Wisconsin's famous extension program. From the very beginning, it was made explicit that correspondence courses "shall not involve the university in any expense." Originally correspondence instruction was conducted under the auspices of the regular faculty although the actual instructional duties were performed by "fellows" and "advanced students." Because of the onerous workload, faculty participation was minimal and enrollment remained small. The effort was revived under President Charles R. van Hise and his new director of extension, Louis E. Reber, two engineers attuned especially to the training needs of industry.

Van Hise had recognized the economic potential of correspondence instruction, judging from the experience of the commercial schools, and he commissioned a study of the for-profit firms. "The enormous success of the commercial correspondence schools suggested that here was an educational opportunity which had been neglected by the Universities," van Hise wrote in 1906. "There are tens of thousands of students in the State of Wisconsin who are already taking correspondence work in private correspondence schools, probably more than thirty thousand, and they are paying for this work outside of the State more than three-quarters of a million dollars per annum."

Up to this point Wisconsin's correspondence courses had offered primarily academic and cultural fare under the auspices of the academic departments, but van Hise, at the behest of businessmen who offered to make donations to the university if it reactivated correspondence study, pushed the enterprise in a decidedly vocational and industrial direction. Reber, formerly the Dean of Engineering at Pennsylvania State University, had the same industrial orientation, viewing correspondence study primarily as a way of providing a trained workforce for industry. "It would be difficult under present conditions to provide a better means for meeting the persistent and growing demand for industrial training than the methods of correspondence study adopted by the University," he observed. "This fact has been cordially recognized and the work encouraged and aided by employers of men wherever it has been established." Before coming to Wisconsin Reber visited the International Correpondence Schools in Scranton and undertook to refashion the Wisconsin correspondence program along the same lines as that leading commercial enterprise.

Reber succeeded in having the correspondence department established independent of the regular faculty, with its own non-academic staff of instructors and with its courses removed from faculty control. Under Reber's direction the Wisconsin correspondence program grew enormously, drawing one of the largest enrollments in the country. The dropout rate was roughly 55 percent and "dropout money" was the name of the game.

Berkeley's program was modelled on Wisconsin's. Initially Berkeley's correspondence courses were meant to be the academic equivalent of resident courses, taught by university faculty and supervised by academic departments, and the university pledged to "place each student in direct personal contact with his instructor." But here too, the program administrators discovered that, as director Baldwin Woods later explained, "correspondence instruction is expensive."

Thus, for economic reasons, the program moved to expand enrollment by catering to the greatest demand, which was for vocational courses for people in business and industry, by engaging in "continuous promotion," employing "field representatives," and relaxing admissions standards ("there is no requirement for admission to a class save the ability to pursue the work with profit"). Enrollment increased fourfold and fees were later increased to whatever the market would bear. Most of the instructional work was done by low-status, part-time "readers" described by one director as "overworked" and who were paid on a piece rate basis of twenty-five to thirty-five cents per lesson. Not surprisingly, the dropout rate averaged 70 to 80 percent. Students were required to pay full tuition up front and a partial refund was allowed only if no more than two lessons had been completed. In 1926 the President's

Report declared that "the fee for a course must be set to bring in income. Expansion must be largely profitable."

At the end of the twenties, after nearly four decades in the business of correspondence instruction, the university-based programs began to come under the kind of scrutiny and scathing criticism heretofore reserved for the commercial schools. The first and most damning salvo came from Abraham Flexner, one of the nation's most distinguished and influential observers of higher education. Best known for his earlier indictment of medical education on behalf of the Carnegie Foundation, Flexner had served for fifteen years as general secretary of the Rockefeller-funded General Education Board and later became the founding director of the Institute for Advanced Study at Princeton. After his retirement from the General Education Board in 1928, Flexner delivered his Rhodes Lectures on the state of higher education in England, Germany, and the United States, which were published in 1930 under the simple title *Universities*.

In his lectures on the situation in the United States, Flexner excoriated the American universities for their commercial preoccupations, for having compromised their defining independence and integrity, and for having thereby abandoned their unique and essential social function of disinterested critical and creative inquiry. At the heart of his indictment was a scornful assessment of university-based correspondence education, focusing in detail upon the academically unseemly activities of the University of Chicago and Columbia University. Flexner acknowledged the social importance of correspondence and vocational education but questioned whether they belonged in a university, where they distracted the institution from its special intellectual mission, compromised its core values, and reoriented its priorities in a distinctly commercial direction. The rush to cash in on marketable courses and the enthusiasm for correspondence instruction, Flexner argued, "show the confusion in our colleges of education with training." The universities, he insisted, "have thoughtlessly and excessively catered to fleeting, transient, and immediate demands" and have "needlessly cheapened, vulgarized, and mechanized themselves," reducing themselves to "the level of the vendors of patent medicines."

He lampooned the intellectually trivial kinds of courses offered by the correspondence programs of Columbia, the University of Chicago, and the University of Wisconsin, and wondered about what would make "a great university descend to such humbug." "What sort of contribution is

Columbia making towards a clearer apprehension of what education really is?", Flexner asked. He particularly decried Columbia's indiscriminate enrollment practices and especially its elaborate and deceptive promotional effort which, he argued, "befuddles the public" and generates a "spurious demand." If Columbia's correspondence courses were genuinely of "college grade" and taught by "regular members of the staff," as Columbia advertised, then why was no academic credit given for them? If correspondence instruction was superior to that of the traditional classroom, then why did not Columbia sell off its expensive campus and teach all of its courses by mail? "The whole thing is business, not education," Flexner concluded. "Columbia, untaxed because it is an educational institution, is in business: it has education to sell [and] plays the purely commercial game of the merchant whose sole concern is profit." Likewise, he bemoaned as "scandalous" the fact that "the prestige of the University of Chicago should be used to bamboozle well-meaning but untrained persons . . . by means of extravagant and misleading advertisements." Finally, Flexner pointed out that regular faculty in most institutions remained justifiably skeptical of correspondence and vocational instruction. The "administrative professoriate," he declared, "is a proletariat."

Flexner's critique of correspondence education, which gained widespread media attention, sent shock waves through academia, prompting internal efforts to raise standards and curtail excessive and misleading advertising. At Columbia, the blow was eventually fatal to the correspondence program. A year after the publication of Flexner's book—and the unveiling of Columbia's ambitious plans for a vastly expanded program with its own grand headquarters—President Butler wrote to his extension director Egbert that "a good many people are impressed unfavorably with our Home Study advertising and continually call my attention to it. I should like to have you oversee this advertising very carefully from the viewpoint of those who criticize it as 'salesmanship,' etc." The result of this belated concern was a severe restriction of advertising (which lasted at Columbia until the late 1960s). The continued unwillingness of Columbia's Administrative Board to grant academic credit for correspondence courses—largely because of the low regard in which these courses were held by the regular faculty—coupled with the restrictions on general advertising, which the board had now come to deem "inappropriate and unwise," effectively undermined the effort to maintain enrollments sufficient to sustain the department (especially in the midst of the Depression) and it was finally officially discontinued in 1937. A year after Flexner's critique, and partly in response to it, the American Association for Adult Education launched a Carnegie Corporation–funded survey of university-based correspondence courses under the direction of Hervey Mallory, long-time head of the Home Study Department at the University of Chicago. Published in 1933 as *University Teaching By Mail*, the study, which generally endorsed and called for the improvement of the correspondence method, acknowledged the validity of much of the criticism.

Referring explicitly to Flexner, the study noted that "many believe that correspondence instruction is not a function of college or university" and wonder "how does it come that literature and art have fallen to the absurd estate of commodities requiring advertisement and postal shipment?" The study argued, however, that while "there is something fine and entirely right in the demand for independence, integrity, and disinterestedness" on the part of universities, the "ideals of practical service, of experiment in educational method, and of participation in the life of the community" are not incompatible with it and insisted that many, especially mature, students had benefitted from correspondence instruction. The study conceded, on the other hand, that "it may be that schoolmen and businessmen have . . . created the demand by a false propaganda of success through education, of promise of additions to the pay envelopes proportional to the number of courses, certificates, credits, and degrees, and other rewards displayed in correspondence study advertising."

In surveying the weaknesses of the method, the study acknowledged the narrowly utilitarian motive and also the "very real isolation" of most correspondence students, owing not only to the intrinsic limitations of the correspondence method of instruction but also to the pressures on instructors that further undermined its promise. "One of the charges against the correspondence study system is that it tends to exploit the student by inducing him to enroll and pay fees, and then fails to give adequate service in return," the study observed; students routinely complained about "insufficient corrections and comments by the instructor" and the "lack of 'personal' contacts with instructors" that contributed to the excessively high dropout rates. In the light of such apparently inescapable weaknesses of correspondence instruction, the authors of the study abandoned altogether earlier evangelical expectations about this new method someday supplanting traditional education and insisted instead, much more modestly, that correspondence instruction should be employed only as a supplement to, rather than a substitute for, classroom instruction. "No reputable proponent of home study seriously suggests that correspondence teaching should replace classroom instruction," the authors declared. "Correspondence study is not advocated as a substitute for campus study, but is established as a supplement with peculiar merits and demerits. Correspondence courses are of the most value to the individual when taken in conjunction with a residence program. They are not a substitute for education. They should not be taken merely in conjunction with one's job or avocation, nor are they to be used simply as a hobby or as an exercise of will power by itself. They serve individual purposes best when they fit into a long-time, socialized program of education." Earlier claims about the alleged superiority of correspondence over classroom instruction were likewise abandoned and various attempts to "experimentally" compare the two were dismissed as scientifically spurious and inconclusive.

The study devoted considerable attention to the unsatisfactory working conditions of instructors—notably that they were overworked and underpaid—in accounting for the failings of the method, which depended ultimately upon "the willingness of the instructor to give a generous amount of attention to the student." "When that fails," the authors noted, "the special merit of the correspondence method, individual instruction, remains individual chiefly on the students' side alone—this is the chief weakness in method—perfunctory reading of reports, lack of helpful suggestions, and delay and neglect by over-burdened" instructors. Instructors excused their perfunctory performance on the grounds that the pay was too small to merit the effort and the authors of the survey confirmed that the workload of instructors was typically excessive and that "the compensation in nearly all the institutions is very small." "The excuse of instructors that pay is too little has some merit. The merit of the excuse lies in the fact that in most cases in the present system the pay is small by the piece, and piecework may be irksome to the teachers both when it is light and when it is heavy, in the first place perhaps because the tangible reward is slight, in the second because the work piles up beyond one's schedule." Most instructors, the study also found, worked on a part-time, fee-for-service basis, with little supervision, which meant both that they suffered from job insecurity and that there was a noticeable "difficulty of maintaining standards." "The employment of readers or graders or fee instructors, as they are variously called, has been severely criticized on the assumption that such readers are not qualified teachers or are doing a merely perfunctory job of paper criticism." "Nearly all university correspondence teachers might be designated as fee instructors," the study found, "since few are on a salary basis."

While the authors of the Carnegie study criticized such pedagogically counterproductive employment practices—and also the "usual policy of the universities not to refund fees" to students who drop out—they placed the blame not so much on the university correspondence programs per se but rather on the commercial pressures with which they were unfairly burdened. "Most university correspondence courses are underfunded and understaffed," they noted, and each is forced to be self-supporting, leaving them no choice but to adopt the unseemly commercial practices of their for-profit cousins. "Correspondence instruction in the university should not be required to 'pay its way' in a business sense any more than classroom instruction," the authors insisted. "The business methods should not be those of a commercial concern whose prime motive is to dispose of commodities or services for a money profit." Yet the survey showed that such was clearly the case. Although the authors warned that no "university correspondence administration should not lay itself open even remotely to objection on grounds of dubious commercial practices, such as 'charging what the traffic will bear,' exacting from students fees that will yield a profit, or giving instructors poor compensation in order to keep costs low," they knew that, given the circumstances in which they were compelled to operate, the circumstances of commodity production, they had no other option.

The belatedly modest and critical tone of the Carnegie survey signaled that the heyday of correspondence education was over. The great expectations of this first foray into the commodification of higher education had been exploded and the movement was spent. Strong criticism of the private, for-profit correspondence schools was ritually repeated over the years, with little noticeable effect, particularly in a series of studies sponsored by the American Council on Education. Likewise, subsequent examinations of university-based correspondence education continued to confirm the findings of the 1933 survey. Thirty years later the General Accounting Office was warning veterans on the GI Bill not to waste their federal funds on correspondence courses. In 1968 the Carnegie-funded Correspondence Education Research Project, which had been commissioned by the National Home Study Council (later renamed the Distance Education and Training Council) and the National University Extension Association, found that correspondence courses suffered from poor quality, perfunctory instructor performance, and a very high dropout rate; that instructors endured low pay (on a piece rate basis) and low status; that programs continued to rely upon "dropout money" to survive; and that there was little prospect for improvement "as long as correspondence instruction is held in such low esteem."

All such investigations and attendant efforts at reform and regulation invariably failed to change the picture, even as correspondence programs adopted the latest media of delivery, including film, telephone, radio, audio-tapes, and television. Universities continued to offer correspondence instruction, of course, but the efforts were much more modest in their claims and ambitions. Poor cousins of classroom instruction, they were for the most part confined to institutionally separate and self-supporting extension divisions and carefully cordoned off from the campus proper, presumably to spare the core institution the expense, the commercial contamination, and the criticism.

Like their now forgotten forebears, today's proponents of distance education believe they are leading a revolution that will transform the educational landscape. Fixated on technology and the future, they are unencumbered by the sober lessons of this cautionary tale or by any understanding of the history they are so busy repeating. If anything, the commercial element in distance education is this time even stronger, heralded anew as a bold departure from tradition. For, now, instead of trying to distinguish themselves from their commercial rivals, the universities are eagerly joining forces with them, lending their brand names to profit-making enterprises in exchange for a piece of the action.

The four institutions examined here as prominent players in the first episode of distance learning are, of course, at it again. The University of Wisconsin has a deal with Lotus/IBM and other private contractors to develop and deliver online distance education, especially under the auspices of its Learning Innovations Center, while the University of California has contracts with America Online and Onlinelearning.net for the same purposes. And the University of Chicago and Columbia are among the most enterprising participants in the new distance education gold rush. The University of Chicago signed a controversial deal with a start-up online education company called UNEXT.com, which is headed by Chicago trustee Andrew Rosenfield and bankrolled in part by junk bond felon Michael Milken. Principal investors in the company include the dean of the law school and two of Chicago's Nobel prize–winning economists. The new game is less about generating revenues from student fees than about reaping a harvest from financial speculation in the education industry through stock options and initial public offerings.

The first university to sign up with UNEXT was Columbia, which has licensed UNEXT to use the school's logo in return for a share in the business. "I was less interested in the income stream than in the capitalization. The huge upside essentially is the value of the equity in the IPO," Columbia's Business School dean, Meyer Feldberg, a friend of Milken's, told the *Wall Street Journal*. "I don't see a downside," he added, betraying an innocence of Columbia's history that would make Flexner roll over in his grave. "I guess our exposure would be if in some way our brand name is devalued by some problem with this experimental venture." Columbia has also set up its own for-profit online distance education company, Morningside Ventures, headed by an executive formerly with the National Football League, satellite, and cable TV companies. Columbia's executive vice president, Michael Crow, explained the need for the company with hyperbole reminiscent of that of his prophesying predecessors in the correspondence movement. "After a thousand years, university-based education is undergoing a fundamental transformation," he declared; "multi-media learning initiatives" are taking us beyond the classroom and the textbook. And he acknowledged the essentially commercial nature of this transformation. "Because of the technologies required and the non-traditional revenue streams involved," he noted, "corporations will play a major role in these new forms of education. We felt the need for a for-profit company to compete effectively and productively."

Last but not least, Columbia has now become party to an agreement with yet another company that intends to peddle its core arts and science courses. Columbia will develop courses and lend its brand name to the company's product line in return for royalties and stock options. According to one source, the company has already been busy recruiting faculty to the enterprise as course developers and has suggested the possibility of using professional actors to deliver them.

For the time being, however, until the actors arrive, the bulk of university-based online distance education courses are being delivered in the same manner as correspondence courses of old, by poorly paid and overworked low-status instructors, working on a per-course basis without benefits or job security and under coercion to assign their rights to their course materials to their employer as a condition of employment. The imperatives of commodity production, in short, are again in full force, shaping the working conditions of instructors until they are replaced once and for all by machines, scriptwriters, and actors.

Just as the promoters of correspondence instruction learned the hard way that the costs of their new methods were much higher than anticipated and that they had to lower their labor costs to turn a profit, so the promoters of online instruction have belatedly discovered that the costs of this latest method are prohibitive unless they likewise reduce their labor costs. As Gregory Farrington, president of Lehigh University, observed recently, "unless the new technologies can be used to increase the average teaching productivity of faculty, there is virtually no chance that those technologies will improve the economics of traditional higher education." But increasing the "teaching productivity of faculty"—whether through job intensification, outsourcing, or the substitution of computers for people—essentially means increasing the number of students per teacher and this invariably results in an undermining of the pedagogical promise of the method, as the experience of correspondence instruction clearly demonstrates. And the degradation of the quality of the education invariably destroys the incentive and motivation of students. Already the dropout rates of online distance education are much higher than those of classroom-based instruction. Finally, as was the case with correspondence courses, it is not possible to receive a bona fide bachelor's degree from a reputable institution through the online medium alone. If online education were truly the equivalent of classroom education, as its proponents suggest, why won't the elite colleges and universities that have so avidly embraced it give full credit for this form of instruction? All rhetoric about the alleged democratization of higher education through online education collapses at this point. Of course, this is the very same challenge Flexner posed for correspondence education.

So here we go again. We have indeed been here before. But there are differences between the current rage for online distance education and the earlier debacle of correspondence distance education. First, the firewalls separating distance education programs from the core campus are breaking down; although they first took hold on the beachheads of extension divisions, commercial online initiatives have already begun to penetrate deeply into the heart of the university. Second, while the overhead for correspondence courses was expensive, the infrastructural expense for online courses exceeds it by an order of magnitude—a technological tapeworm in the guts of higher education. Finally, while correspondence programs were often aimed at a broad market, most efforts remained merely regional. The ambitious reach of today's distance educators, on the other hand, is determinedly global in scale, which is why the World Trade Organization is currently at work trying to remove any and all barriers to international trade in educational commodities. In short, then, the dire implications of this second distance education craze far outstrip those of the first. Even if it fails to deliver on its economic and pedagogical promises, as it surely will, its promoters will push it forward nevertheless, given the investment entailed, leaving a legacy of corruption and ruin in its wake. In comparing Napoleon III with Napoleon I, Karl Marx formulated his famous dictum "first time tragedy, second time farce." A comparison of the past and present episodes of distance education suggests perhaps a different lesson, namely, that sometimes the tragedy follows the farce.

2

The Coming of the Online University

I n the course of 1997 events at two large North American universities signalled dramatically that we were entering a new era in higher education, in which the halls of academe would rapidly be drawn into the age of automation. In midsummer the UCLA administration launched its historic "Instructional Enhancement Initiative" requiring computer websites for all of its arts and sciences courses by the start of the fall term, the first time that a major university has made mandatory the use of computer telecommunications technology in the delivery of higher education. At the same time, moreover, UCLA began offering online courses in collaboration with a for-profit company, the Home Education Network (THEN), that was created for this purpose and is now headed by a former UCLA vice chancellor.[1]

Earlier, in the spring of 1997, the full-time faculty of Canada's third largest university—York University in Toronto—ended an historic two-month strike having secured for the first time anywhere formal contractual protection against precisely the kind of administrative action being taken by UCLA. The unprecedented faculty job action, the longest university strike in Canadian history, was taken partly in response to unilateral administrative initiatives in the implementation of instructional technology, the most egregious example of which was an official solicitation to private corporations inviting them to permanently place their logo on a university online course in return for a $10,000 contribution to courseware development. As at UCLA, the York University administration helped create a private entity, Cultech, directed by the vice president for research and several deans and dedicated, in collaboration with a consortium of private sector firms, to the commercial development and exploitation of online education.

---

1. Developments at UCLA are discussed further in Chapters Three and Five of this volume.

Significantly, at both UCLA and York, the presumably cyber-happy students clearly indicated their own lack of enthusiasm for the prospect of a high-tech academic future, recommending against the initiative at UCLA and at York lending their support to striking faculty and launching their own independent investigation of the commercial, pedagogical, and ethical implications of online educational technology. In fall 1997 the student handbook distributed annually to all students by the York Federation of Students contained a warning about the dangers of online education.

Thus, at the very outset of this new age of higher education, the lines were drawn in the struggle that will ultimately determine its shape. On the one side university administrators and their myriad commercial partners, on the other those who constitute the core relation of education: students and teachers. (The chief slogan of the York faculty during the strike was "the classroom vs. the boardroom.") It is no accident, then, that the high-tech transformation of higher education was initiated and implemented from the top down, either without any student and faculty involvement in the decision making or despite it. At UCLA the administration launched their initiative during the summer when many faculty are away and there was little possibility of faculty oversight or governance; faculty were thus left out of the loop and kept in the dark about the new web requirement until the last moment. And UCLA administrators also went ahead with its initiative, funded by a new compulsory student fee, despite the formal student recommendation against it. Similarly the initiatives of the York administration in the deployment of computer technology in education were taken without faculty oversight and deliberation, much less student involvement.

What drives this headlong rush to implement new technology with so little regard for deliberation of the pedagogical and economic costs and at the risk of student and faculty alienation and opposition? A short answer might be the fear of getting left behind, the incessant pressures of "progress." But there is more to it. For the universities were not simply undergoing a technological transformation. Beneath that change, and camouflaged by it, lies another: the commercialization of higher education. For here as elsewhere technology is but a vehicle and a disarming disguise.

The major change to befall the universities over the last two decades has been the identification of the campus as a significant site of capital accumulation, a change in social perception that has resulted in the systematic con-

version of intellectual activity into intellectual capital and, hence, intellectual property. There have been two general phases of this transformation. The
first, which began twenty years ago and is still under way, entailed the commodification of the research function of the university, transforming scientific and engineering knowledge into commercially viable proprietary products that could be owned and bought and sold in the market. The second,
which we are now witnessing, entails the commodification of the educational function of the university, transforming courses into courseware, the
activity of instruction itself into commercially viable proprietary products
that can be owned and bought and sold in the market. In the first phase the
universities became the site of production and sale of patents and exclusive
licenses. In the second, they are becoming the site of production of—as well
as the chief market for—copyrighted videos, courseware, CD-ROM's, and
websites.

The first phase began in the mid-1970s when, in the wake of the oil crisis
and intensifying international competition, corporate and political leaders of
the major industrialized countries of the world recognized that they were losing their monopoly over the world's heavy industries and that, in the future,
their supremacy would depend upon their monopoly over the knowledge that
had become the lifeblood of the new so-called knowledge-based industries
(space, electronics, computers, materials, telecommunications, and bioengineering). This focus upon "intellectual capital" turned their attention to the
universities as its chief source, implicating the universities as never before in
the economic machinery. In the view of capital, the universities had become
too important to be left to the universities.

Within a decade there was a proliferation of industrial partnerships and
new proprietary arrangements, as industrialists and their campus counterparts invented ways to socialize the risks and costs of creating this knowledge
while privatizing the benefits. This unprecedented collaboration gave rise to
an elaborate web of interlocking directorates between corporate and academic boardrooms and the foundation of joint lobbying efforts epitomized by the
work of the Business–Higher Education Forum. The chief accomplishment of
the combined effort, in addition to a relaxation of antitrust regulations and
greater tax incentives for corporate funding of university research, was the
1980 reform of the patent law, which for the first time gave the universities
automatic ownership of patents resulting from federal government grants.
Laboratory knowledge now became patents, that is, intellectual capital and

intellectual property. As patent-holding companies, the universities set about at once to codify their intellectual property policies, develop the infrastructure for the conduct of commercially viable research, cultivate their corporate ties, and create the mechanisms for marketing their new commodity, exclusive licenses to their patents. The result of this first phase of university commodification was a wholesale reallocation of university resources toward its research function at the expense of its educational function.

Class sizes swelled, teaching staffs and instructional resources were reduced, salaries were frozen, and curricular offerings were cut to the bone. At the same time, tuition soared to subsidize the creation and maintenance of a commercial infrastructure (and correspondingly bloated administration) that has never really paid off. In the end students were paying more for their education and getting less, and the campuses were in crisis.[2]

The second phase of the commercialization of academia, the commodification of instruction, is touted as the solution to the crisis engendered by the first. Ignoring the true sources of the financial debacle—an expensive and low-yielding commercial infrastructure and greatly expanded administrative costs—the champions of computer-based instruction focus their attention rather upon increasing the efficiencies of already overextended teachers. And they ignore as well the fact that their high-tech remedies are bound only to compound the problem, increasing further, rather then reducing, the costs of higher education. (Experience to date demonstrates clearly that computer-based teaching, with its limitless demands upon instructor time and vastly expanded overhead requirements—equipment, upgrades, maintenance, and technical and administrative support staff—costs more not less than traditional education, whatever the reductions in direct labor; hence the need for outside funding and student technology fees.) Little wonder, then, that teachers and students are reluctant to embrace this new panacea. Their hesitation reflects not fear but wisdom.[3]

---

2. Tuition began to outpace inflation in the early 1980s, at precisely the moment when changes in the patent system enabled the universities to become major vendors of patent licenses. According to data compiled by the National Center for Educational Statistics, between 1976 and 1994 expenditures on research increased by 21.7 percent at public research universities while expenditure on instruction decreased by 9.5 percent. Faculty salaries, which had peaked in 1972, fell precipitously during the next decade and have since recovered only half the loss.

3. Recent surveys of the instructional use of information technology in higher education clearly indicate that there have been no significant gains in either productivity improvement or pedagogical enhancement. Kenneth C. Green, director of the Campus Computing Project, which conducts annual surveys of information technology use in higher

But this second transformation of higher education is not the work of teachers or students, the presumed beneficiaries of improved education, because it is not really about education at all. That's just the name of the market. The foremost promoters of this transformation are rather the vendors of the network hardware, software, and "content"—Apple, IBM, Bell, the cable companies, Microsoft, and the edutainment and publishing companies Disney, Simon and Schuster, Prentice-Hall, et al.—who view education as a market for their wares, a market estimated by the Lehman Brothers investment firm to be potentially worth several hundred billion dollars. "Investment opportunity in the education industry has never been better," one of their reports proclaimed, indicating that this will be "the focus industry" for lucrative investment in the future, replacing the health care industry. (The report also forecasts that the educational market will eventually become dominated by EMOs—education maintenance organizations—just like HMOs in the health care market.) It is important to emphasize that, for all the democratic rhetoric about extending educational access to those unable to get to the campus, the campus remains the real market for these products, where students outnumber their distance-learning counterparts six to one.

In addition to the vendors, corporate training advocates view online education as yet another way of bringing their problem-solving, information-processing, "just-in-time" educated employees up to profit-making speed. Beyond their ambitious in-house training programs, which have incorporated computer-based instructional methods pioneered by the military, they envision the transformation of the delivery of higher education as a means of supplying their properly prepared personnel at public expense.

The third major promoters of this transformation are the university administrators, who see it as a way of giving their institutions a fashionably forward-looking image. More importantly, they view computer-based instruction as a means of reducing their direct labor and plant maintenance costs—fewer teachers and classrooms—while at the same time undermining

---

education, noted that "the campus experience over the past decade reveals that the dollars can be daunting, the return on investment highly uncertain." "We have yet to hear of an instance where the total costs (including all realistically amortized capital investments and development expenses, plus reasonable estimates for faculty and support staff time) associated with teaching some unit to some group of students actually decline while maintaining the quality of learning," Green wrote. On the matter of pedagogical effectiveness, Green noted that "the research literature offers, at best, a mixed review of often inconclusive results, at least when searching for traditional measures of statistical significance in learning outcomes."

the autonomy and independence of faculty. Additionally, they are hoping to get a piece of the commercial action for their institutions or themselves, as vendors in their own right of software and content. University administrators are supported in this enterprise by a number of private foundations, trade associations, and academic-corporate consortia that are promoting the use of the new technologies with increasing intensity. Among these are the Sloan, Mellon, Pew, and Culpepper foundations, the American Council on Education, and, above all, Educom, a consortium representing the management of 600 colleges and universities and a hundred private corporations.

Last but not least, behind this effort are the ubiquitous techno-zealots who simply view computers as the panacea for everything, because they like to play with them. With the avid encouragement of their private sector and university patrons, they forge ahead, without support for their pedagogical claims about the alleged enhancement of education, without any real evidence of productivity improvement, and without any effective demand from either students or teachers.

In addition to York and UCLA, universities throughout North America are rapidly being overtaken by this second phase of commercialization. These have included the stand-alone virtual institutions like the University of Phoenix, the wired private institutions like the New School for Social Research, the campuses of state universities such as the University of Maryland and the new Gulf Coast campus of the University of Florida (which boasts no tenure). On the state level, the states of Arizona and California initiated their own statewide virtual university projects, while a consortia of western "smart states" have launched their own ambitious effort to wire all of their campuses into an online educational network. In Canada, a national effort was spearheaded by the Telelearning Research Network centered at Simon Fraser University in Vancouver, with the aim of bringing most of the nation's higher education institutions into a "Virtual U" network.

The overriding commercial intent and market orientation behind these initiatives was made explicit in the most ambitious US effort to date, the Western Governors' Virtual University Project. Its stated goals were to "expand the marketplace for instructional materials, courseware, and programs utilizing advanced technology," "expand the marketplace for demonstrated competence," and "identify and remove barriers to the free functioning of these markets, particularly barriers posed by statutes, policies, and administrative rules and regulations." "In the future," Utah governor Mike Leavitt proclaimed, "an institution of higher education will become a little like a local television station." Start-up funds for the project come from the private sector, specifically from Educational Management Group, the educational arm of the world's largest educational publisher, Simon and Schuster, and the proprietary impulse behind their largesse was made clear by Simon and Schuster CEO Jonathan Newcomb: "The use of interactive technology is causing a fundamental shift away from the physical classroom toward anytime, anywhere learning—the model for postsecondary education in the twenty-first century." This transformation is being made possible by "advances in digital technology, coupled with the protection of copyright in cyberspace."

Similarly, the national effort to develop the "Virtual U" customized educational software platform in Canada has been directed by an industrial consortium that includes Kodak, IBM, Microsoft, McGraw-Hill, Prentice-Hall, Rogers Cablesystems, Unitel, Novasys, Nortel, Bell Canada, and MPR Teltech, a research subsidiary of GTE. The commercial thrust behind the project is explicit here too. Predicting a potential fifty-billion-dollar Canadian market, the project proposal emphasizes the adoption of "an intellectual property policy that will encourage researchers and industry to commercialize their innovations" and anticipates the development of "a number of commercially marketable hardware and software products and services," including "courseware and other learning products." The two directors of the project, Simon Fraser University professors, have formed their own company to peddle these products in collaboration with the university. At the same time, the nearby University of British Columbia spun off the private WEB-CT company to peddle its own educational website software, WEB-CT, designed by one of its computer science professors and subsequently used by UCLA. Soon after, WEB-CT entered into production and distribution relationships with Silicon Graphics and Prentice-Hall and fast became a major player in the American as well as Canadian higher education market. By the beginning of the fall term of 1997, WEB-CT licensees included, in addition to UCLA and California State University, the universities of Georgia, Minnesota, Illinois, North Carolina, and Indiana, and such private institutions as Syracuse, Brandeis, and Duquesne.

The implications of the commodification of university instruction are twofold in nature, those relating to the university as a site of the production of the commodities and those relating to the university as a market for them.

The first raises for the faculty traditional labor issues about the introduction of new technologies of production. The second raises for students major questions about costs, coercion, privacy, equity, and the quality of education.

With the commodification of instruction, teachers as labor are drawn into a production process designed for the efficient creation of instructional commodities, and hence become subject to all the pressures that have befallen production workers in other industries undergoing rapid technological transformation from above. In this context faculty have much more in common with the historic plight of other skilled workers than they care to acknowledge. Like these others, their activity is being restructured, via the technology, in order to reduce their autonomy, independence, and control over their work and to place workplace knowledge and control as much as possible into the hands of the administration. As in other industries, the technology is being deployed by management primarily to discipline, deskill, and displace labor.

Once faculty and courses go online, administrators gain much greater direct control over faculty performance and course content than ever before and the potential for administrative scrutiny, supervision, regimentation, discipline and even censorship increase dramatically. At the same time, the use of the technology entails an inevitable extension of working time and an intensification of work as faculty struggle at all hours of the day and night to stay on top of the technology and respond, via chat rooms, virtual office hours, and e-mail, to both students and administrators to whom they have now become instantly and continuously accessible. The technology also allows for much more careful administrative monitoring of faculty availability, activities, and responsiveness.

Once faculty put their course material online, moreover, the knowledge and course design skill embodied in that material is taken out of their possession, transferred to the machinery and placed in the hands of the administration. The administration is now in a position to hire less skilled, and hence cheaper, workers to deliver the technologically prepackaged course. It also allows the administration, which claims ownership of this commodity, to peddle the course elsewhere without the original designer's involvement or even knowledge, much less financial interest. The buyers of this packaged commodity, meanwhile, other academic institutions, are able thereby to contract out, and hence outsource, the work of their own employees and thus reduce their reliance upon their in-house teaching staff.

Most important, once the faculty converts its courses to courseware, their services are in the long run no longer required. They become redundant, and when they leave, their work remains behind. In Kurt Vonnegut's classic novel *Player Piano* the ace machinist Rudy Hertz is flattered by the automation engineers who tell him his genius will be immortalized. They buy him a beer. They capture his skills on tape. Then they fire him. Today faculty are falling for the same tired line, that their brilliance will be broadcast online to millions. Perhaps, but without their further participation. Some skeptical faculty insist that what they do cannot possibly be automated, and they are right. But it will be automated anyway, whatever the loss in educational quality. Because education, again, is not what all this is about; it's about making money. In short, the new technology of education, like the automation of other industries, robs faculty of their knowledge and skills, their control over their working lives, the product of their labor, and, ultimately, their means of livelihood.

None of this is speculation. In the fall of 1997 the UCLA faculty, at administration request, dutifully or grudgingly (it doesn't really matter which) placed their course work—ranging from just syllabi and assignments to the entire body of course lectures and notes—at the disposal of their administration, to be used online, without asking who will own it much less how it will eventually be used and with what consequences. At York University, some untenured faculty have been required to put their courses on video, CD-ROM, or the Internet or lose their job. They have then been hired to teach their own now automated course at a fraction of their former compensation. The New School in New York now routinely hires outside contractors from around the country, mostly unemployed Ph.D.'s, to design online courses. The designers are not hired as employees but are simply paid a modest flat fee and are required to surrender to the university all rights to their course. The New School then offers the course without having to employ anyone. And this is just the beginning.

Educom, the academic-corporate consortium, now renamed Educause, established their Learning Infrastructure Initiative that same year, which included the detailed study of what professors do, breaking the faculty job down in classic Taylorist fashion into discrete tasks, and determining what parts can be automated or outsourced. Educom believes that course design, lectures, and even evaluation can all be standardized, mechanized, and consigned to outside commercial vendors. "Today you're looking at a highly personal human-mediated environment," Educom president Robert Heterich observed. "The potential to remove the human mediation in some areas and replace it with automation—smart, computer-based, network-based systems—is tremendous. It's gotta happen."

Toward this end, university administrators are coercing or enticing faculty into compliance, placing the greatest pressures on the most vulnerable—untenured and part-time faculty, and entry-level and prospective employees. They are using the academic incentive and promotion structure to reward cooperation and discourage dissent. At the same time they are mounting an intensifying propaganda campaign to portray faculty as incompetent, hidebound, recalcitrant, inefficient, ineffective, and expensive—in short, in need of improvement or replacement through instructional technologies. Faculty are portrayed above all as obstructionist, as standing in the way of progress and forestalling the panacea of virtual education allegedly demanded by students, their parents, and the public.

The York University faculty had heard it all. Yet still they fought vigorously and ultimately successfully to preserve quality education and protect themselves from administrative assault. During their long strike they countered such administration propaganda with the truth about what was happening to higher education and eventually won the support of students, the media, and the public. Most important, they secured a new contract containing unique and unprecedented provisions that, if effectively enforced, give faculty members direct and unambiguous control over all decisions relating to the automation of instruction, including veto power. According to the contract, all decisions regarding the use of technology as a supplement to classroom instruction or as a means of alternative delivery (including the use of video, CD-ROM's, Internet websites, computer-mediated conferencing, etc.) "shall be consistent with the pedagogic and academic judgements and principles of the faculty member employee as to the appropriateness of the use of technology in the circumstances." The contract also guarantees that "a faculty member will not be required to convert a course without his or her agreement." Thus, the York faculty will be able to ensure that the new technology, if and when used, will contribute to a genuine enhancement rather than a degradation of the quality of education, while at the same time preserving their positions, their autonomy, and their academic freedom. The battle is far from won, but it is a start.

The second set of implications stemming from the commoditization of instruction involve the transformation of the university into a market for the commodities being produced. Administrative propaganda routinely alludes to an alleged student demand for the new instructional products. At UCLA officials are betting that their high-tech agenda will be "student driven," as students insist that faculty make fuller use of the website technology in their courses. To date, however, there has been no such demand on the part of students, no serious study of it, and no evidence for it. Indeed, the few times students have been given a voice, they have rejected the initiatives hands down, especially when they were required to pay for it (the definition of effective demand, i.e. a market). At UCLA, students recommended against the Instructional Enhancement Initiative. At the University of British Columbia, home of the WEB-CT software being used at UCLA, students voted in a referendum four-to-one against a similar initiative, despite a lengthy administration campaign promising them a more secure place in the high-tech future. Administrators at both institutions have tended to dismiss, ignore, or explain away these negative student decisions, but there is a message here: students want the genuine face-to-face education they paid for, not a cyber-counterfeit. Nevertheless, administrators at both UCLA and UBC decided to proceed with their agenda anyway, desperate to create a market and secure some return on their investment in the information technology infrastructure. Thus, they are creating a market by fiat, compelling students (and faculty) to become users and hence consumers of the hardware, software, and content products as a condition of getting an education, whatever their interest or ability to pay. Can all students equally afford this capital-intensive education?

Another key ethical issue relates to the use of student online activities. Few students realize that their computer-based courses are often thinly veiled field trials for product and market development, that while they are studying their courses, their courses are studying them. In Canada, for example, universities have been given royalty-free licenses to Virtual U software in return for providing data on its use to the vendors. Thus, all online activity including communications between students and professors and among students are monitored, automatically logged and archived by the system for use by the vendor. Students enrolled in courses using Virtual U software are in fact formally designated "experimental subjects." Because federal monies were used to develop the software and underwrite the field trials, vendors were compelled to comply with ethical guidelines on the experimental use of human subjects. Thus, all students, once enrolled, are required to sign forms releasing ownership and control of their online activities to the vendors. The form states, "As a student using Virtual U in a course, I give my permission to have the computer-generated usage data, conference transcript data, and virtual artifacts data collected by the Virtual U software . . . used for research, development, and demonstration purposes."

According to UCLA's Home Education Network president John Kobara, all of their distance-learning courses are likewise monitored and archived for use by company officials. On the UCLA campus, according to Harlan Lebo of the provost's office, student use of the course websites will be routinely audited and evaluated by the administration. Marvin Goldberg, designer of the UCLA WEB-CT software, acknowledges that the system allows for "lurking" and automatic storage and retrieval of all online activities. How this capability will be used and by whom is not altogether clear, especially since websites are typically being constructed by people other than the instructors. What third parties (besides students and faculty in the course) will have access to the student's communications? Who will own student online contributions? What rights, if any, do students have to privacy and proprietary control of their work? Are they given prior notification as to the ultimate status of their online activities, so that they might be in a position to give, or withhold, their informed consent? If students are taking courses that are just experiments, and hence of unproven pedagogical value, should students be paying full tuition for them? And if students are being used as guinea pigs in product trials masquerading as courses, should they be paying for these courses or be paid to take them? More to the point, should students be content with a degraded, shadow cyber-education? In Canada student organizations have begun to confront these issues head on, and there are some signs of similar student concern emerging also in the United States.

In his classic 1959 study of diploma mills for the American Council on Education, Robert Reid described the typical diploma mill as having the following characteristics: "no classrooms," "faculties are often untrained or nonexistent," and "the officers are unethical self-seekers whose qualifications are no better than their offerings." It is an apt description of the digital diploma mills in the making. Quality higher education will not disappear entirely, but it is bound to become the exclusive preserve of the privileged, available only to children of the rich and the powerful. For the rest of us a dismal new era of higher education has dawned. In future years we will look upon the wired remains of our once great democratic higher education system and wonder how we let it happen. That is, unless we decide now not to let it happen.

3

The Battle over Intellectual Property Rights

The commodification of higher education depends upon the ability of university administrators to buy and sell the educational offerings of faculty. This ability presupposes, however, the transformation of long-established academic traditions and rights. Above all, administrators have had to challenge and usurp the faculty's legal right to ownership of the copyright to their course materials—an endeavor which has sparked the central battle over the future of academia.

For most of the last two decades this transformation has centered upon the research function of the universities. But it has now shifted to the instructional function. The primary commercial impulse has come from non-academic forces, industrial corporations seeking indirect public subsidy of their research needs and private vendors of instructional hardware, software, and content looking for subsidized product development and a potentially lucrative market for their wares. In both cases, there has been a fundamental transformation of the nature of academic work and the relationship between higher educational institutions and their faculty employees.

The commercialization of research entailed the conversion of the intellectual process of research into discrete products—inventions—and the conversion of these inventions into commodities—something that could be owned and exchanged on the market—by means of patents and exclusive licenses. With this change, faculty who conducted research in the service of their role as educators and scholars became instead producers of commodities for their employer. Universities could become commercial players not only because they were the major site of federally funded scientific and technological research but also because amendments to the patent law had given academic contractors ownership of all patents resulting from federally funded research. This potentially gave the universities something to trade with industry: licenses to those patents. But before the universities could make any proprietary deals with industry they had first to secure the patent rights of their research faculty and staff, because patents are issued only to inventors, not to institutions. Universities thus established ad hoc arrangements with their own professors, giving them a share of revenues in exchange for their patent rights. Eventually, they adopted formal intellectual property policies similar to those devised many decades before by private industry: employees would be required contractually to assign their patent rights to the university as a routine condition of employment.

In the process, research, formerly pursued as an end in itself or as a contribution to human knowledge, now became a means to commercial ends and researchers became implicated, directly or indirectly and wittingly or not, in the business of making money for their universities. The commercialization of academic research brought universities and industry into close partnership; it made some people very rich and no doubt resulted in the development of some new technologies. But it also ushered in a brash new regime of proprietary control, secrecy, fraud, theft, and commercial motives and preoccupations. Some argue that this new commercial ethos has irreversibly corrupted the university as a site of reliably independent thought and disinterested inquiry, placing in jeopardy a precious and irreplaceable public resource.

Current moves to commercialize the instructional activities of the universities follow a similar pattern. Here the instructional process, classroom teaching, is converted into products, such as a CD-ROM's, websites, or courseware. These products are then converted into marketable commodities by means of copyrights and licenses to distribute copyrighted instructional products. Like the commercialization of research, the commercialization of instruction entails a fundamental change in the relationship between the universities and their faculty employees. Here faculty who develop and teach face-to-face courses as their primary responsibility as educators are transformed into mere producers of marketable instructional commodities that they may or may not themselves "deliver."

Universities today are going into business for themselves, as the producers and distributors of commercial instructional products, or they are making deals with private firms for the production and distribution of online courses. But before the universities can begin to trade on their courses, they must first control the copyright to course material. Course copyright is the sine qua non of the digital diploma mill. In copyright law, however, ownership follows authorship. This means that course materials are the property of the teaching faculty and staff who developed them. Traditionally, universities have acknowledged that faculty, as the authors of courses, have owned their course materials and hence copyright to them (except in those cases where extraordinary university resources were involved in course development, which might entail shared ownership). But the universities are now undertaking to usurp such traditional faculty rights in order to capitalize on the online instruction marketplace, and it is for this reason that the rather arcane matter of copyright and intellectual property has become the most explosive campus issue of the day. It is here that the battle line over the future of higher education has been drawn.

For faculty and their organizations it is a struggle not only over proprietary control of course materials per se but also over their academic role, their autonomy and integrity, their future employment, and the future of quality education. In the wake of the online education gold rush, many have begun to wonder, will the content of education be shaped by scholars and educators or by media businessmen, by the dictates of experienced pedagogy or a quick profit? Will people enroll in higher educational institutions only to discover that they might just as well have stayed home watching television?

Since the mid-90s the universities have been actively experimenting with solutions to their copyright dilemma. By early 1998 several universities had entered into formal agreements with private firms, giving some indication of where they were headed: UCLA and the Home Education Network (THEN); UC Berkeley and America On Line (AOL); and the University of Colorado and Real Education. These documents, heretofore confidential, herald the dawning of a new regime of instruction. The agreements show that university administrators and corporate investors knew from the start that control over intellectual property—and not how to spread the benefits of technology —was the heart of the matter.

The initial loci of these arrangements were the extension programs of the universities, the testing grounds for online instruction and the beachheads, so to speak, for the commercialization of higher education. In each of these contracts, entered into without faculty knowledge, much less approval, the university has explicitly assumed its own, rather than faculty, authorship/ownership of course materials, in violation not only of academic tradition but perhaps also of federal copyright law. In claiming authorship/ownership as a precondition of making the deal, the universities might also have committed fraud. Whether or not the universities overstepped legal boundaries, it is clear that there was a move afoot to establish surreptitiously a new practice, a new tradition, in which universities automatically own all rights to course material developed by faculty. In this context, faculty confront the need to act quickly to assert and confirm their rightful claim to their course materials, as their inaction might retrospectively be seen by the courts as a tacit acknowledgment of the abandonment of those rights. In the longer run, universities will no doubt undertake to routinize this theft by requiring faculty to assign all copyrights on course material to the university as a condition of employment, as they have done with patents.

An early initiative in this direction was the secret agreement between UCLA and the Home Education Network (THEN) signed on June 30, 1994, and amended February 21, 1996. This agreement entailed the granting by a university of exclusive production and distribution rights to electronic courses, including copyright, to a private, for-profit corporation, without any prior faculty consultation or approval.

THEN emerged not from the world of education but from the fast-hustle media world of spins and sound bites, cable TV and public relations. It was the brainchild of political media consultant and television producer Alan Arkatov, who produced and marketed the media campaigns of over a dozen US senators, governors, and mayors before serving as senior advisor to President Clinton's 1992 campaign chairman, Mickey Kantor. In 1994 he negotiated a landmark contract with the Regents of the University of California to form an unprecedented arrangement with UCLA Extension (UNEX), the largest continuing higher education program in the country. The agreement gave Arkatov exclusive rights to all electronic delivery of UNEX courses and the exclusive use of the UCLA name for that purpose, thereby launching THEN as "the most comprehensive continuing distance learning program of its kind in the United States."

THEN is now directed by its president and CEO, John Kobara, who comes out of the cable television industry and the public relations and marketing side of academia. A UCLA graduate, Kobara was vice president and general manager of Falcon TV, one of the nation's largest independent cable operators, and served as president of the Southern California Cable Association before returning to UCLA to direct the alumni association. By the time he joined THEN in 1997, Kobara was UCLA's vice chancellor of university relations, directing all of the university's public relations, marketing, and government and alumni relations activities. Combining their media experience, political influence, and insider knowledge of UCLA and its myriad community connections, Arkatov and Kobara were well placed to make the most profitable use of their ambitious arrangement with UCLA. But UCLA administrators, meanwhile, had ambitions of their own, not only to provide a new revenue stream for UNEX but to establish it, and UCLA, as the premier vehicle for distance learning in the University of California system, and beyond.

The extremely broad agreement between THEN (signed by Arkatov) and the Regents of the University of California (on behalf of UNEX, a part of the Division of Continuing Education of UCLA, signed by Robert Lapiner, UCLA Dean of Continuing Studies) granted to THEN the exclusive right to produce, for a ten-year "production period," and exploit, in perpetuity, all electronic versions of UNEX courses: "the sole, exclusive and irrevocable right under copyright and otherwise to make, produce and copyright by any means or 'Technology,' as such term is hereinafter defined, now known or hereafter devised during the 'Production Period,' as such term is hereinafter defined, audio, visual, audio/visual, digital and/or other recordings of all UNEX classes. . . ." as well as "the sole, exclusive and irrevocable right under copyright and otherwise to exhibit, perform, broadcast, transmit, publish, reproduce, manufacture, distribute, advertise, sell, rent, lease, market, publicize, promote, merchandise, provide technical support for, license and otherwise exploit, generally deal in and with and turn to account the recordings by all means and technology and in all media and forms of expression and communication now known or later developed in all languages throughout the universe (the 'Territory') in perpetuity. . . ." THEN also secured the right to use the "University of California" and "UCLA" names in connection with the exploitation of their rights granted in the agreement, as well as the right to assign or transfer their interests in the agreement to "any entity."

In consideration of this generous grant of rights, UNEX would receive a percentage of THEN's gross receipts (increasing from 6 to 12 percent over the course of the term) plus reimbursement of expenses incurred in the preparation of courses, including materials and wages. UNEX retained the right to designate which courses would or would not be converted to electronic form and the right to final approval of their content. However, it agreed that "THEN shall have the unlimited right to vary, change, alter, modify, add to and/or delete from the Recordings, and to rearrange and/or transpose the Recording and change the sequence thereof." In 1995 there was apparently some difference of opinion between the parties over whether or not the 1994 agreement covered online and Internet delivery of courses. THEN insisted that it did and ultimately prevailed upon UCLA to formally amend the agreement, stipulating explicitly that "UNEX and THEN acknowledge that the inclusion of On-Line Rights is on the same economic and other terms as pertain to Recordings in the Agreement and that all such terms shall be interpreted so as to encompass On-Line Rights."

If the THEN-UCLA agreement brought the pecuniary preoccupations of private commerce into the heart and soul of higher education, it also carried with it another characteristic aspect of proprietary enterprise: secrecy. Despite, or perhaps because of, the broad terms and far-reaching implications of their agreement, THEN officials and UCLA administrators formally agreed to keep it secret. In a confidentiality clause in the 1994 agreement, it was agreed that "except as required by law, UNEX shall hold in confidence and shall not disclose or reveal to any person or entity confidential information relating to the nature and substance of this Agreement . . ." and that any participating "Instructor shall hold in confidence and not disclose or reveal to any person or entity confidential information relating to the nature and substance of the agreement between UNEX and THEN. . . ." While THEN clearly had proprietary motives for such confidentiality, why did UCLA administrators, trustees of a public institution trading in publicly created goods, agree to such secrecy? What did the university have to hide? Perhaps it was what the agreement had to say about its larger ambitions, and, especially, its relations with faculty.

Kobara maintained that this arrangement was a modest one, restricted to UNEX and thus without any significance, or any reason for concern, beyond it. He insisted that THEN had no relationship with UCLA but only with UNEX. According to him, UNEX is an independent entity. This is not the case. While UNEX is self-supporting, it is unambiguously a part of UCLA, as the agreement itself makes clear. It was for this reason that an officer of UCLA, Robert Lapiner, signed the agreement, representing the Regents. Moreover, Kobara's modesty is clearly belied by the agreement, which reveals intentions of a much wider scope. According to the agreement, "The parties contemplate that the relationship with THEN may extend to other University of California campuses. Because of UNEX's unique responsibility to be bound to THEN for the Term hereof, THEN agrees that the participation of all other University of California campuses as well as other academic units of UCLA in this project will be coordinated by UNEX and for the purposes of this Agreement shall be considered 'UNEX Classes.' An appropriate share of revenues otherwise payable to UNEX for any such courses shall, however, be distributed proportionately to the participating University of California campus or other academic unit of UCLA." Whether or not they are able to realize their grand vision, it is clear that UCLA from the outset intended to extend its distance education operations beyond UNEX and, through UNEX—the largest continuing education program in the UC system—beyond UCLA to other UC campuses.

In the fall of 1997 the UCLA Division of Letters and Science launched its Instructional Enhancement Initiative mandating that every course must have a website containing at a minimum course outlines and assignments and encouraging faculty to put their lectures and other materials online as well. Like the THEN-UCLA deal, this action was taken without debate or formal faculty approval. THEN and UCLA officials maintained that there was no connection between this unprecedented initiative and their UNEX activities. In response to increasingly apparent faculty concern, UCLA's provost of Arts and Letters, Brian Copenhaver, subsequently distributed a letter to all faculty insisting, perhaps too much, that IEI is "resolutely and only academic" and that "there are no plans to use IEI commercially." Reading the agreement, however, one had to wonder.

At the heart of the THEN-UCLA deal is the crucial matter of copyright. As is typical in any such agreement, the parties have to attest to the fact that they indeed have the right and authority to grant whatever it is they are granting. Thus, UNEX affirmed that "UNEX has the full right, power, and authority to enter into and perform this Agreement and to grant to and vest in THEN all rights herein set forth, free and clear of any and all claims, rights, and obligations whatsoever." Under this assumption, UNEX agreed that "As between UNEX, THEN, and the instructors of the UNEX Classes (the 'Instructors'), THEN shall be the owner of all right, title, and interest, including without limitation, the copyright, in and to all Recordings of UNEX Classes produced by and for THEN hereunder and, for purposes of Title 17 of the United States Code also known as the Copyright Act of 1976, as amended (the 'Copyright Act'), THEN shall be deemed the author of the Recordings." By what legal right and under what authority could UNEX make such a grant, given the fact that the instructors who create the courses rather than UCLA or UNEX are the rightful and heretofore acknowledged owners of copyright? The instructors, of course, were never even party to this agreement. This was the crux of the agreement and all such arrangements.

In order to be in a position to uphold its side of the bargain, UNEX formally agreed that it would undertake to compel its instructors, on THEN's behalf, to assign their copyrights to UNEX, thereby enabling UNEX to assign them to THEN. This was made fully explicit with the inclusion in the agreement of an "Exhibit A," outlining a compulsory "Instructors' Agreement," whereby instructors would be made to surrender their rights to UNEX as a condition of employment. The agreement stipulated that "UNEX shall use its best efforts to cause each Instructor to agree in writing ('Instructor Agreement') for the specific stated benefit of THEN, to the provisions set forth on Exhibit 'A' attached hereto." Furthermore, the agreement stipulated that any such instructor agreement had to meet the specifications not only of UNEX but also of THEN, which "shall have the right of prior written approval of the form and substance of the agreements entered into by UNEX and Instructors concerning the production and exploitation of the Recordings."

Exhibit A is a five-page document that specifies in detail what the instructor must give up and do for UNEX and THEN in order for UNEX to meet its contractual obligations to THEN. Predictably, the instructor must agree to grant to UNEX the same rights granted by UNEX to THEN, namely "the sole, exclusive and irrevocable right under copyright and otherwise to make, produce and copyright by any means or technology now known or hereafter devised Recordings of all UNEX Classes taught by Instructor" as well as "the sole, exclusive and irrevocable right under copyright and otherwise to exhibit, perform, broadcast, transmit, publish, reproduce, manufacture, distribute, advertise, sell, rent, lease, market, publicize, promote, merchandise, provide technical support for, license and otherwise exploit, generally deal in and with and turn to account the Recordings by all means and technology and in all media and forms of expression and communication now known or later developed in all languages throughout the Territory in perpetuity." The instructor must acknowledge and agree that "THEN shall be deemed the author of the Recordings" and that the "Instructor has no rights of any kind or nature in the Recordings of UNEX Classes taught by the Instructor"; and must "forever waive any right to assert any rule, law, decree, judicial decision or administrative order of any kind throughout the world, which allows Instructor any right in the moral rights (*droit moral*) in the Recordings."

According to Exhibit A, the "Instructor must not permit the Course Materials utilized by the Instructor for UNEX Classes taught during the Production Period to be recorded by any Technology, except by THEN" unless it is approved by THEN or is restricted to publication in print form on paper (e.g. books). The instructor is also obligated to assist UNEX and THEN in securing releases to all copyrighted material used in the instructor's course. And just as UNEX must use its best efforts to cause the instructor to sign the instructor agreement, so the "Instructor shall use Instructor's best efforts to cause all guest lecturers taking part in UNEX Classes taught by such Instructor to execute agreements approved by UNEX and THEN that are consistent with the balance of the provisions of Exhibit A." Finally, the instructor is required to execute any other documents consistent with the terms of the instructor agreement, as requested by UNEX or THEN, and if the instructor fails to do so, "the Instructor shall be deemed to have appointed UNEX and/or THEN as Instructor's irrevocable attorney-in-fact with full power of substitution and delegation and with full and complete right and authority . . . to perform such acts and take such proceedings in the name of Instructor . . . "

The instructor agreement, a formal written contract between employee and employer in which employee rights are legally transferred to the employer, was seen by the parties in 1994 as the way UNEX would secure the power and authority required to comply with its agreement with THEN, at the expense of the instructors. By early 1998, however, both parties contended that such instructor agreements were no longer necessary. According to the terms of a revised agreement, which they were then still in the process of finalizing, the actual ownership of electronic courses would reside solely with UNEX while THEN would merely have exclusive rights of distribution. And UNEX maintained that its ownership rights are automatic and would not require any formal contract with their employees. As David Menninger, UCLA's Associate Dean of Continuing Education and UCLA Extension, explained to me in a letter in December 1997, "since the focus of the Extension/THEN relationship has shifted to Extension online courses, for which the Regents of the University of California retain ownership, no such instructor's agreement has ever been used, nor is any further need anticipated."

It is not clear upon what legal basis Menninger asserts his claim that the Regents of the University of California retain ownership, given the traditional legal rights of the instructors to these courses. According to Kathy

Whenmouth, technology transfer specialist in the University of California's President's Office, the university does not yet have any policy on the copyright of online course materials. Clearly, the matter is far from settled. What exactly are the rights of instructors and the Regents? Now that the UNEX-THEN agreement has seen the light of day, it will no doubt become a focus of controversy. Is it legal? Will it withstand a legal challenge? Whatever the ultimate legal status of the agreement, which would have to be determined in court, this episode sheds much light upon the methods, intentions, and visions of those involved in the commodification and commercialization of university instruction.

The second agreement, between America on Line (AOL) and UC Berkeley (the Regents of the University of California), points in much the same direction. Signed on July 26, 1995, this agreement, which also contains a confidentiality clause, centered upon Berkeley's extension program, the Center for Media and Independent Learning. Here the arrangement from the outset entailed only the licensing of course distribution rights without any transfer of copyright from the university to the company. According to the agreement, the university aims to offer "electronic courses in a broad spectrum of disciplines (Arts and Humanities, Business and Management, Computer Science, Hazardous Materials Management, Natural Sciences, Social Sciences), for credit or for professional development." Accordingly, the "University grants AOL a non-exclusive, revocable, worldwide license to market, license, distribute, and promote" these courses. In doing so, the "university represents and warrants to AOL" that such offerings "will not infringe on or violate any copyright, patent or any other proprietary right of any third party." Once again, as was the case with the UCLA-THEN agreement, the university represented to AOL that it alone owned the course materials and that no third parties, including the faculty who develop courses, had any rights to them. In order to secure faculty compliance with this claim, the university drew up a generic course development "letter of agreement" for instructors to execute. In this document, which instructors were required to sign, the university informed instructors that "The Regents of the University of California will own the copyright to all materials you develop, in print or other media, for use in this UC Extension course . . . and we retain the right to continue offering the course should you resign as instructor." By means of this contract the university would obtain, and the instructors abandon, ownership of all course materials. Instructors are paid a modest "honorarium" for developing the course and abandoning their rights, payable half on acceptance of the materials and half on actual delivery of the course. Whereas AOL receives 10 percent of all royalty revenues, the instructors receive none.

The final example is possibly the most far-reaching, involving the Denver-based company Real Education, Inc. (Real Ed) and the entire University of Colorado. Real Education was founded in 1996 by CEO Rob Helmick, an attorney and former general counsel for various universities who specialized in education law and the "merger and acquisition of educational institutions worldwide." In 1996 Helmick's law firm, Helmick and Associates International, acquired Real Information Systems, one of the leading worldwide web production companies in the United States, and created Real Education, Inc., "so that universities could easily outsource instruction." Real Education has become a major player in the outsourcing of university online instruction and currently has contracts with some twenty universities and colleges throughout the United States, including the University of Colorado, Northern Illinois University, Rogers University, and the Colorado Community Colleges. The company specializes in providing universities with all of the hardware, software, Internet links and technical support they need for online course delivery, including assistance with course development. By 1998 it was collaborating with Microsoft and Simon and Schuster with the aim of creating a standard for the industry. For its part, the University of Colorado was in the forefront of online education, having won the Eddy Award of the National Science Foundation as the "Number One Online University in the World."

After some preliminary collaboration, Real Ed and the University of Colorado entered into a formal agreement on May 27, 1997. The arrangement engages Real Ed to provide the technical means for online course development and delivery but the university retains all copyright to course material. According to the agreement, the "University, on behalf of its four campuses, wishes to develop its online capability utilizing Real Ed's Einstein Network Version 2.5 (or the latest version thereof) to create University credit and non-credit courses for delivery in the United States and abroad." As part of its obligations, Real Ed agrees to "oversee the adaptation of existing distance-learning courses and collaborate with the University's faculty and staff in the development of new courses" and to "provide instructional design support to

University faculty to assist in the transfer of lectures to the online format." However, according to the contract, "it is understood and agreed that the relationship of University and Real Ed, with respect to all course development, is that of author and editor, final approval and ownership rights over University-developed material will vest in the University. . . ." Once again, in making a deal with a private firm, the university explicitly identifies itself as the "author" of all course materials having full "ownership rights."

Having made clear its proprietary claims vis-à-vis Real Ed, the university also made an effort to establish the contractual basis for such claims vis-à-vis its faculty. The university has drawn up an "Agreement for Development of Courses Between the Regents of the University of Colorado and Faculty Course Developer" to be signed by all faculty developing online courses. According to this agreement, "Faculty acknowledges that the online course is deemed as a 'work made for hire' within the meaning of the US Copyright Act of 1976 and the Board of Regents of the University of Colorado shall own exclusively and forever all rights thereto including derivative works." In addition, "Faculty acknowledges and agrees that the 'on-line' course itself may not be used in faculty consulting, in delivering lectures or presentations to another academic institution, and may not be duplicated or distributed to other individuals, academic institutions or corporations without a written agreement and approval of the University."

In return for developing a typical three-credit course and assigning copyright on all course materials to the university, the faculty member receives $1,000 plus royalties of 10 percent of revenues up to $125,000 and 15 percent thereafter. (Real Ed receives $5,000 for each course developed plus $100 per student.) At that stage, faculty involvement in online course development was voluntary. However, according to the agreement with Real Ed, the university has the power to designate which faculty will develop such courses. According to Maureen Schlenker of the University of Colorado at Denver, who oversees "UC Online," departments might require faculty to participate. No doubt untenured and part-time instructors, those with the least job security and lowest pay, will most likely be pressed into service. Marvin D. Loflin, dean of the College of Arts and Sciences on the Denver campus, says he is considering plans to hire non-professorial "teaching associates" to teach online courses. "I'm prepared to make over the whole infrastructure of higher education," he proclaimed in the *Chronicle of Higher Education* of March 27, 1998.

These agreements herald a new regime in higher education, one that is taking hold of the nation's campuses at an accelerating rate: the commodification and commercialization of instruction. Extension programs are the cutting edge for this new commercial ethos not only because of their obvious involvement in distance learning but also because they are typically staffed by the most vulnerable instructors, people who have little job security and would thus be most ready to comply with university demands. But as the arrangement between the University of Colorado and Real Ed makes especially clear, the new regime of online education extends far beyond university extension programs and the most vulnerable. Indeed, it is now becoming increasingly apparent that the real market for online courses will be the on-campus population, as the experience of the University of Colorado already indicates. And as UCLA's Instructional Enhancement Initiative makes plain, faculty at all levels will ultimately be drawn into the new regime, through encouragement or coercion. The implications of these agreements therefore must be considered seriously by anyone who is using or plans to use electronic means to enhance or deliver their courses. Who owns the material you have placed on the website or e-mail? Without a clear and definitive assertion of copyright claims by faculty, the universities may be able to usurp such rights by default.

Without control over copyright there is no clear way forward for the universities and their corporate partners. The CEO of Simon and Schuster, Jonathan Newcomb, made this point clearly: commercial online education presupposes "advances in digital technology coupled with the protection of copyright in cyberspace." In this context, moves by faculty to resist administration appropriation of their copyright—through collective bargaining, litigation, or direct action—has become essential for the preservation of their legal rights, their autonomy, their jobs, and, above all, the quality and integrity of higher education.

4

The Bloom Is Off the Rose

Far sooner than most observers might have imagined, the juggernaut of online education appeared to stall. For the first few years after the pioneering initiatives to take higher education online were announced, it seemed there was no stopping it. Promoters of instructional technology and "distance learning" advanced with ideological bravado as well as institutional power, the momentum of human progress allegedly behind them. They had merely to proclaim "it's the future" to throw skeptics on the defensive and convince seasoned educators that they belonged in the dustbin of history. The monotonal mantras about our inevitable wired destiny, the prepackaged palaver of silicon snake-oil salesmen, echoed through the halls of academe, replete with sophomoric allusions to historical precedent (the invention of writing and the printing press) and sound bites about the imminent demise of the "sage on the stage" and "bricks and mortar" institutions. Only a year or two later, however, the wind was out of their sails, their momentum broken, their confidence shaken.

At countless campus forums on the subject throughout North America, the burden of proof was shifting from the critics to the promoters. Though still amply funded and politically supported, they had increasingly been put on the defensive. This is not to say that the pressures behind the online university had abated but that, ideologically at least, the terrain had changed irreversibly. By the end of 1998 promoters of the online university were compelled to try to buttress their still lame arguments with half-baked data about pedagogical usefulness, economic return, or market demand. Attendance at campus events multiplied by an order of magnitude as faculty and students finally become alert to the administrative agendas and commercial con games behind this seeming technological revolution.

Off campus, the scene was much the same. Study after study seemed to confirm that computer-based instruction reduces performance levels and that habitual Internet use induces depression. Advertisers were peddling platinum MasterCards and even Apple laptop computers by subtly acknowledging that "seven days without e-mail" is "priceless" and that being in touch with your office from anywhere anytime is a "bummer." Meanwhile, all the busy people supposedly clamoring for distance learning—who allegedly constitute the multibillion-dollar market for cyberinstruction—are curling up at night with *Tuesdays with Morrie*, a sentimental evocation of the intimate, enduring, and life-enriching relationship between a former student and his dying professor, now four years on the *New York Times* bestseller list. "Have you ever really had a teacher? One who saw you as a raw but precious thing, a jewel that, with wisdom, could be polished to a proud shine? If you are lucky enough to find such teachers, you will always find your way back." So much for distance learning.

Above all, a specter came to haunt the high-tech hijackers of higher education, the specter of faculty (and student) resistance. The series on which this book is based began with the juxtaposition of two events from 1997. The first, UCLA's Instructional Enhancement Initiative (and partnership with the Home Education Network), signaled the commodification of instruction and commercialization of higher education by means of digital technology. The second, the unprecedented two-month strike by faculty at York University, represented the first significant sign of opposition to this new regime and the unholy alliance among academic administrators and their myriad corporate and political partners. These events had the effect of drawing the lines along which the struggle over the future of the university would be waged. Within a year or so, that struggle had intensified beyond anyone's expectations.

At UCLA, the widely touted Instructional Enhancement Initiative, which mandated websites for all 3800 arts and sciences courses, floundered in the face of faculty recalcitrance and resistance. By the end of the first academic year, only 30 percent of the faculty had put any of their course material online and several dozen had actively resisted the initiative and the way it had been unilaterally inspired and implemented. UCLA Extension's partnership with the Home Education Network (which changed its name in the spring to Onlinelearning.net) ran aground on similar shoals when instructors made it clear that they would refuse to assign any of their rights in their course materials to either UCLA (the Regents) or the company. In already up to their necks, the partners decided simply to claim the rights anyway and proceed apace, flying without wings on borrowed time.

The strike at York awakened the faculty there to a new vigilance and militancy with regard to the computer-based commercialization of the university. It also emboldened others elsewhere. At Acadia University, for example, which had linked up with IBM in hopes of becoming the foremost wired institution in Canada, the threat of a faculty strike forced the administration to back off from some of their unilateral demands for online instruction, and faculties at other Canadian institutions have been moving in the same direction. Even within Simon Fraser University's Department of Communications, home of the recently refunded Canadian flagship Telelearning Research Center, serious faculty challenges to the virtual university enterprise have emerged and gone public.

In the United States as well, resistance was on the rise. Faculty and students in the California State University system, the largest public higher educational institution in the country, fought vigorously and effectively against the California Educational Technology Initiative (CETI), an unprecedented deal between CSU and a consortium of firms (Microsoft, GTE, Hughes, and Fujitsu), which would have given them a monopoly over the development of the system's telecommunications infrastructure and the marketing and delivery of CSU online courses. Students resisted being made a captive market for company products while faculty responded to the lack of faculty consultation and threats to academic freedom and their intellectual property rights. In particular, they feared that CETI might try to dictate online course content for commercial advantage and that CSU would appropriate and commercially exploit their course materials.

Throughout the CSU system, faculty senates passed resolutions against CETI, tried to obtain an injunction to stop the deal, and used the media and public forums to campaign against it. Together with students, faculty participated in widely publicized demonstrations; at Humboldt State University in northern California, students demonstrating against the deal altered the sign at the campus entrance to read "Microsoft University," a creative act of defiance which caught the attention of media around the country. Through the efforts of the Internet activist group NetAction, the controversy over the CETI deal became a cause célèbre, galvanizing opposition and leading to high-profile government hearings and legislative scrutiny and skepticism. Opposition to the deal from California-based business competitors such as Apple, Netscape, and Sun (none of the CETI partners were California-based) also contributed to the erosion of legislative support. (The deal may also have been unconstitutional under state law.) Before long, Microsoft and Hughes dropped out, then GTE, and the deal was dead. Any new deal would be sure to encounter determined and well-organized opposition.

Further north at the University of Washington in Seattle, a campus with little recent history of faculty activism, four hundred faculty members attended a February 1998 forum on "digital diploma mills" sponsored by the local chapter of the AAUP. Later that spring, Washington governor Gary Locke and Wallace Loh, his chief advisor on higher education, gave speeches extolling the virtues of the "brave new world of digital education" and outlined plans for statewide initiatives in that direction. The AAUP immediately drafted an open letter to the governor vigorously opposing this vapid vision and circulated it among the faculty. Within two days, seven hundred faculty from across the campus, from Slavic studies to computer science, had signed the letter. Another two hundred signatures were later added and the letter was made public in early June. Within a week, this bold and eloquent faculty protest had made headlines around the country.

"We feel called upon to respond before quixotic ideas harden into disastrous policies," the faculty wrote the governor. "While costly fantasies of this kind present a mouth-watering bonanza to software manufacturers and other corporate sponsors, what they bode for education is nothing short of disastrous. . . . Education is not reducible to the downloading of information, much less to the passive and solitary activity of staring at a screen. Education is an intersubjective and social process, involving hands-on activity, spontaneity, and the communal experience of sharing in the learning enterprise. . . . We urge you to support learning as a human and social practice, an enrichment of soul and mind, the entitlement of all citizens in a democracy, and not a profit-making commodity to be offered on the cheapest terms to the highest bidder. The University of Washington is a vital resource to our community, not a factory, not a corporation, not a software package. Its excellence and integrity are not only assets that we as a community can afford to maintain, but also assets that we cannot afford to squander."

The widespread academic and media support engendered by this letter compelled the governor to meet with a faculty delegation and ultimately to retreat somewhat from fully embracing the virtual education agenda, at least temporarily. "We're not unique," history professor Jim Gregory, one of the organizers of the letter campaign, told the press. "We just may be a little more mobilized at this particular moment." He was right. All the way at the other end of the continent, near Ft. Myers, Florida, similar sentiments were emerging. The Florida Gulf Coast University (FGCU), the new tenth campus of the state higher education system, was advertised as the "university of the future," "built as a testing-ground for Internet-based instruction," where faculty are hired on short-term contracts without a tenure system. Not long after the University of Washington protest the FGCU faculty and their union, the United Faculty of Florida, began openly to question the pedagogical value of online education, to protest against the increased workload entailed in distance learning, to resist the university's attempt to appropriate their intellectual property, and to lobby for a standard tenure system rather than have to reapply for their jobs every two years.

In an administration survey, more than half of the faculty—who were hired on the understanding that the new campus would specialize in distance education—opposed increasing the proportion of distance-learning classes from 16 to 25 percent of classes. "Some professors say they remain unconvinced of the method's effectiveness," the *Wall Street Journal* reported in July 1998. The questionable economic viability of existing distance education classes has also been an issue.

"Some observers say significant savings can be achieved only if the size of distance-learning classes increases," the newspaper reported, but enlarging the classes only undermines the pedagogical promise even more. Intellectual property issues were at the center of faculty concerns. Faculty became especially alarmed when the dean of Instructional Technology, Kathleen Davie, was quoted in a *Chronicle of Higher Education* article saying that, with regard to faculty course materials, "the first rights belong to the university." A new draft policy on intellectual property, formulated without faculty involvement by Davie and her associates, is explicit on this point: "IP developed by FGCU employees (faculty, staff, and students) under university sponsorship or with university support shall belong to the university. University sponsorship or support means the work is conceived or reduced to practice: as a result of the employee's duties; through the use of university resources, such as facilities or equipment; or with university funds, or funds under the control of or administered by the university." In a response to a faculty member's query about this, Dean Davie summed up the university position: "For the most part, the university holds the copyrights for instructional materials created as part of one's compensated workload."

The creator of one course has already complained about the university's efforts to seek outside sponsorship without his permission. Chuck Lindsay, the president of the FGCU Faculty Senate, noted in a letter to the *Chronicle of Higher Education* that the faculty had not been involved in the formulation of the policy and emphasized that "we do not subscribe to the notion that online course materials are, as such, a product of work for hire. . . . We hold that any policy that attempts to lay down across-the-board levels of ownership and revenue sharing for new online course materials reflects a perspective that ascribes an inferior status to original instructional creations and a work for hire mentality; both are contrary to the mission and guiding principles of FGCU."

FGCU is not alone in moving in this direction, of course; draft policies of the University of California, the University of Victoria, the University of Kansas, and Penn State, to name a few, reflect similar intent. But here the unionized faculty have kept themselves abreast of the situation, have gone public with their concerns, and have begun to mobilize their resources for the struggle. The administration is on the defensive. In an interview this summer, Dean Davie acknowledged that she had personally declined a faculty request that I be invited to the campus to hold a forum on these issues, out of fear of jeopardizing her position.

The faculty actions at CSU, the University of Washington, and FGCU were not isolated events. The ferment throughout academia became apparent at the international Digital Diploma Mills conference held at Harvey Mudd College in Claremont, California, in April 1998. The conference attracted well-informed faculty and student participants and an audience of campus activists and rank-and-file union members from throughout the United States and Canada, as well as Mexico. (The keynote speaker was Mary Burgan, general secretary of the AAUP, who suggested that "distance makes the heart grow colder.") The two days of sessions critically examined the political economy, pedagogical value, and economic viability of online education and explored the implications for faculty and students, while those in attendance used their free time to compare notes, make contacts, and extend their networks. The *Chronicle of Higher Education* ran a two-page story on the conference, which ended on a revealing note, pointing out that "officials at Harvey Mudd took pains to distance themselves from the event."

At the same time, faculty and student activists have been holding similar forums on their own campuses. I myself have participated in many such events at campuses including the University of Pittsburgh, Alma College, James Madison University, Embry-Riddle University, George Mason University, the University of Western Ontario, the University of Wisconsin, the University of Washington, the California State University campuses in Sacramento and San Bernardino, California Polytechnic University in Pomona, and the University of California campuses at Irvine and Los Angeles. At all of these events it has become clear that faculty and students alike were realizing that this was a moment of reckoning, a "high noon" for higher education. They were overcoming their traditional timidity and parochialism to make common cause with like-minded people across the continent, to fight for their own and the larger public interest against the plans and pronouncements of peddlers and politicians who in general know little about education. Having learned that they are not alone, faculty found new confidence in their own experience and expertise, and in their rightful capacity to decide what is a good education. Socrates, they reminded themselves, was not a content provider.

In the wake of this resistance, the media caught the scent, publicly validating and magnifying its message. After several years of puff pieces and press releases about the wonders of wired learning, the media began to give the matter more scrutiny and critics their due. "Virtual Classes Trend Alarms Professors," the *New York Times* reported in June 1998; a front page article in the *Wall Street Journal* in August carried the headline "Scholarly Dismay: College Professors Balk at Internet Teaching Plans"; describing what it called the "backlash against virtual education," the *Christian Science Monitor* carried another summer story entitled "Professors Peer Doubtfully into a Digital Future"; the *Industry Standard*, "The Newsmagazine of the Internet Economy," began its feature article "Academics Rebel Against an Online Future" with the words: "Hell no—we won't go—online. . . . The backlash has begun."

The *San Francisco Chronicle*, the *Seattle Times*, the *Los Angeles Times*, the *Boston Globe*—all ran critical articles examining the commodification and commercialization of university instruction. In June 1998 the *Industry Standard*'s cover story was "Ideas for Sale: Business is racing to bring education online. Now academics fear they're becoming just another class of content provider." The headline for the article read "Higher Earning: The Fight to Control the Academy's Intellectual Capital." In response to the open letter to the governor from University of Washington faculty that same month, the *Seattle Times* ran an editorial entitled "Potential Pitfalls," noting that "Signs of high tech corporate corruption are already sneaking into higher education classrooms." Indeed.

If the media-anointed "backlash" against virtual education has prompted a bit more skepticism on the part of reporters and editorial writers, so too has the pitiful performance of the virtuosi themselves, whose market appears to have been a mirage. After several years of high-profile hype and millions of dollars, the flagship Western Governors' Virtual University opened for business this fall, offering hundreds of online courses. Expecting an initial enrollment of 5000, the WGU enrolled only 10 people, and received just 75 inquiries. Intended to put a positive spin on this disaster, WGU marketing director Jeff Edward's double-talk unwittingly hit the nail on the head: "it points out that students are pretty serious about this." Serious enough, that is, to know crap when they see it.

It was much the same story at Onlinelearning.net, the UCLA partner that described itself as "one of the leading global suppliers of online continuing education." The company lost two million dollars in its first year of business and was unable to pay UCLA the anticipated royalties. According to insiders, it was then losing about $60,000 a month. John Kobara, the president of the company and former UCLA vice chancellor for marketing, acknowledged at a company event in November 1998 that it was indeed a very risky business. Kobara noted that most apparent successes are misleading: at the universities of Colorado, Washington, and Arizona the great majority of alleged "distance-learning" customers "are in the dorms" while most online programs, such as those at Berkeley and Vanderbilt, have retention rates of well less than 50 percent. "Retention is the challenge," Kobara explained. Getting people enrolled is one thing, and difficult enough. Getting them to remain enrolled and complete their courses is another thing entirely. The *New York Times* of November 2 confirmed that these were not isolated experiences in an article entitled "More Colleges Plunging Into Uncharted Waters of On-Line Courses."

Distance-learning administrators kept their chins up and issued upbeat press releases that became increasingly hard to believe. Officials at WGU, the Southern Regional Electronic Campus (SREC), which coordinates distance learning courses in sixteen southern states, and the California Virtual University, which coordinates the online offerings of one hundred California campuses, all expressed optimism about the future of distance learning. "We feel confident that there is tremendous interest, especially in the non-traditional student environment," said WGU's Jeffrey Xouris. "Figures indicate significant interest in distance education," said CVU's Rich Halberg. "The dirty little secret," Gerald Heeger, dean of Continuing and Professional Studies at NYU, told the *New York Times*, "is that nobody's making any money."

In each case the basic story was the same: great expectations have yielded great expenditures. The high-tech hallucinations of new revenue streams that so enchanted administrators everywhere were conjured up by voodoo demographics, which mistook distance for demand. What was left out of the equation was whether or not people, on the basis of convenience and computer gimmickry, would be willing to pay more for less education.

In time-honored fashion, the purveyors of this dismal product turned to the taxpayer to bail them out. They placed their bets on the Distance Education Demonstration Program contained in the education bill approved by Congress and signed by Bill Clinton in late 1998. This bill waives classroom requirements for federal student aid eligibility for distance learning customers, thereby priming the distance education market and providing an indirect subsidy to vendors. According to existing law, students had to spend a specified number of hours in a classroom to be eligible for student aid. Vendors had been lobbying for some time, against strenuous opposition from traditional academic institutions and unions, for a waiver of such requirements, which would render their customers eligible for student aid and them eligible for a handsome handout.

The new legislation granted such a waiver for fifteen organizations engaged exclusively in distance learning, including the Western Governors' University. But, even fattened with such pork, it was by no means assured that the distance-learning market would materialize on anything like the scale dreamed up by the wishful thinkers of Wall Street. An inflated assessment of the market for online distance education was matched by an abandonment of financial common sense, as officials recklessly allocated millions of (typically taxpayer) dollars toward untested virtual ventures.[1] Suckered by the siren songs and scare tactics of the silicon snake-oil salesmen, university and college officials have thrown caution to the wind and failed to full-cost their pet projects. Former chief university financial officer Christopher Oberg warned at the Harvey Mudd conference that administrators had suspended normal

---

1. See Chapter Six below for further developments in the tale of public money spent to bail out the cause of private profit from higher education.

accounting practices at their peril. (Little wonder that the presumably more sober Certified Public Accounts Review program at Northern Illinois University broke off its partnership with online vendor Real Education, citing questionable business practices.)

In the face of faculty and student resistance, increasing media skepticism, and notably lackluster performance, some university administrators began to break ranks. It is perhaps no surprise to hear a note of caution emanating from an elite private institution, which must retain some semblance of genuine education for its privileged clientele even while competing for their favors with high-wire acts. Yet it is nevertheless remarkable to find it coming from one of the nation's premier technical institutions, which famously foisted all of this technology upon us in the first place. Last year Michael Dertouzos, director of MIT's Laboratory for Computer Science—home of the World Wide Web—waxed eloquent about the virtues of non-virtual education. "Education is much more than the transfer of knowledge from teachers to learners. As an educator myself, I can say firsthand that lighting the fire of learning in the hearts of students, providing role models, and building student-teacher bonds are the most critical factors for successful learning. These cardinal necessities will not be imparted by information technology. . . . [T]eachers' dedication and ability will still be the most important educational tool." And now, Dertouzos's boss, MIT president Charles Vest, has added his voice to the chorus. "Even though I'm from MIT, I'm not convinced technology is the answer to everything," Vest conceded. In particular, the relationship between teacher and student "is an experience you can never replace electronically." Echoes of Tuesdays with Morrie.

More striking still was the inaugural address of J. Bernard Machen as president of the University of Utah. The University of Utah is located in Salt Lake City, the headquarters of the WGU, and among the distinguished guests at the inauguration was Utah governor and WGU co-chairman Michael Leavitt, who once proclaimed that "in the future an institution of higher education will become a little like a local television station." Formerly the provost at the University of Michigan, Machen forcefully decried the vocational emphasis on online learning and the shifting allocation of public higher education resources toward virtual instruction at the expense of traditional campus-based education. "Let us not succumb to the temptation to force a college education to its lowest common denominator," Machen insisted. "It inherently limits the broader, more interactive aspects of a university education. Spontaneous debate, discussion, and exchange of ideas in the classroom are essential in developing the mind. Poetry must be heard, interpreted and discussed, with professors and classmates. Learning about the different professions and academic disciplines available at the University of Utah requires personal involvement, and that is only available on our campus, and it can only be experienced by being here. . . . The kind of education I am describing is not the cheapest, but it is the best."

Predictably, Machen's remarks were derisively dismissed by Governor Leavitt's office. "It is not the first time that we have heard a kind of fearful, skeptical reaction of the higher education community," one aide to the governor remarked, in a condescending manner all too familiar to faculty critics. But they were not listening carefully, for this is not what they had heard before. No longer were students and faculty (and the rare administrator) speaking up for quality education out of fear and defensiveness in the face of a preordained and prematurely foreclosed virtual future. Emboldened by recent experience (and forewarned by the disastrous demise of public health care), their voices now took on new-found conviction and resolve. The tide had turned. Indeed, it is now the tired response of the governor's office that appears time-worn and out of touch, the damning words strangely hollow without the weight of history behind them. The bloom is off the rose.

5

Fool's Gold:
Confronting Reality at UCLA

n January 1998, a controversy erupted at UCLA over its relationship with a private company, The Home Education Network (THEN), with which it was engaged in the delivery of distance education. The controversy was prompted by disclosure in the earliest of the articles in this *Digital Diploma Mills* series, and subsequent media coverage, of some of the details of the arrangement, by that time already five years in the making but still relatively unknown on the UCLA campus. Two days after the appearance of an article on the deal in the *Los Angeles Times*, Robert Lapiner, UCLA's dean of Continuing Studies and University Extension (UNEX), wrote a letter to the newspaper's editor. Lapiner clarified that THEN was not a part of UCLA but an independent privately capitalized company, and UNEX was not UCLA but rather an independent self-supporting division of UCLA. He maintained that the UNEX-THEN relationship was sound and beneficial.

The very next day, however, Lapiner sent off a dispatch to Julie Gordon at the University of California Office of the President, copied to UCLA's chancellor, Albert Carnesale, that suggested a different tale. Lapiner urged that his response to the *LA Times* be circulated "for the sake of damage control," and acknowledged that "this affair is not going to go away." Here Lapiner conceded that there had indeed been problems with the relationship and he sought to reassure the chancellor, who had only recently assumed office, that these problems would not tarnish the reputation of UCLA as a whole and were being remedied. "From the outset of our relationship with THEN," Lapiner wrote, "I put in a firewall between Extension and the rest of the campus, so that whatever might go wrong (and much has) in the relationship, it would not impact others' initiatives or strategic interests. Indeed, I tried to reenforce that firewall over the last couple of years, but for reasons outside of UNEX's span of control our bargaining power was egregiously compromised." Lapiner emphasized that earnest efforts were underway "to protect the university from greater risk and to fix something we didn't break." A short while later Lapiner told an Academic Senate subcommittee looking into the matter that, while he himself had serious reservations about some key aspects of the collaborative arrangement, "I was told to sign it anyway." He did not reveal who gave the order.

At the end of his letter to the *LA Times*, Lapiner complained that the newspaper had failed to try to get a full picture of the arrangement and noted cryptically that "there's a compelling story about public-private relationships here." This chapter is a belated attempt to tell that story. It is based upon a review of several thousand pages of documents obtained from UCLA under the California Public Records Act as well as conversations with some of the principal participants. It is offered as a cautionary tale, an example not simply of university-based distance education but, more significantly, of the private commercial hijacking of public higher education via distance education. It examines the current craze for distance education from the perspective not of technology but of political economy, and shifts our attention for a moment from the machinery to the machinations. In particular, it examines in detail, by way of a case study, the great expectation of financial returns—fueled by extravagant technological fantasies—that underlies much of today's enthusiasm for distance education. This expectation, and the corollary pursuit of what appears increasingly to be little more than fool's gold, has already led to a worrisome relaxation of sound financial management practice and legal safeguards of the public interest, a bending of the rules of established procedure, and quite possibly even the breaking of the law.

The collaboration between public higher education institutions and private for-profit companies, as in the development and delivery of online instruction, entails an encounter between two fundamentally different cultures and betrays an increasing academic enchantment with the entrepreneurial ethos of the commercial world, a deference to and awe of, and a naive impulse to emulate, the risks and *realpolitik* of business (using public money and resources) and a corresponding sacrifice of the core values that define universities as unique and invaluable. This sacrifice entails a loss not merely to the universities but, more important, to the public that sustains them and depends upon them.

The relationship between UCLA and THEN (later renamed Onlinelearning. net —OLN) emerged out of joint discussions begun in January 1993, exactly five years before the controversy about it erupted. THEN was the brainchild of Alan Arkatov, a TV producer and political media consultant who enjoyed very close ties to the entertainment industry and higher Democratic Party circles. As vice president of the political media consulting firm Doak, Shrum, and Associates, Arkatov had worked on myriad Democratic mayoral, gubernatorial, and senatorial campaigns and, in 1992, served as senior advisor to Mickey Kantor, chairman of the Clinton presidential campaign. In establishing his company, therefore, Arkatov was able to draw upon what Lapiner admiringly referred to as his "connections."

One of the early important associates of THEN, for example, was Charles Manatt, whom Arkatov described as a "lifelong friend." Manatt was the former chairman of the Democratic National Committee, head of the Southern California Democratic Party, and co-chair of the Clinton-Gore campaign. He was also a member of the Board of Governors of the UCLA Foundation. From the start, THEN was represented by Manatt's law firm, Manatt and Phelps, a major player in the entertainment industry. Another key participant was Arkatov's "friend" Ralph Ochoa, an influential attorney, political lobbyist, and deal broker who had been a member of the University of California Board of Regents in his capacity as head of the University of California Alumni Association. Like Manatt, Ochoa also sat on the Board of Governors of the UCLA Foundation and was, in addition, a member of UCLA's Board of Trustees and Board of Visitors. Ochoa enjoyed considerable influence in the office of the UCLA chancellor.

From the outset, the association with UCLA was the sine qua non for the new company. Arkatov sought to build his private firm upon the taxpayer-created foundation of UCLA's brand name and curriculum; the initial focus was UCLA Extension, the nation's largest university extension progam, but Arkatov envisioned an expanded relationship with all of UCLA, and, eventually, with the entire University of California system. His plans took shape in January 1993—the same month he filed the incorporation papers for the new firm—in discussions with Lapiner, to whom he was introduced through Ochoa. Thus, the initiation of the relationship with UCLA and the establishment of THEN took place more or less at the same time.

Arkatov proposed to UCLA that he would develop the means of distributing UNEX courses electronically beyond the classroom, via video (and later online), in exchange for exclusive electronic rights to all UNEX courses. His success was due as much to his connections with the UCLA administration as to the intrinsic virtues of his proposal. At the heart of the effort, as he well understood, was the securing of exclusive rights to the intellectual property embodied in course material, for commercial exploitation. The title of his company prospectus made clear the nature of the enterprise: "UCLA Extension via Multimedia: Education as a Business."

On the UCLA side, enthusiasm for the proposal stemmed from the expectation of enormous financial returns that Arkatov had kindled, a growing emphasis upon entrepreneurial efforts within the university at a time of fiscal restraint, and an awe of the real-world power and glamour of the entertainment industry. University officials wanted to be seen as players in this high-stakes world, to be taken seriously, to show that they too had the vision and the guts to make it big. Accordingly, UCLA granted Arkatov the exclusive rights he sought and adopted the posture of a venture capital operation, expending public funds and offering THEN the use of its public resources in anticipation of a windfall. UCLA appears to have afforded Arkatov privileged use of the UCLA brand name, access to its marketing and publication facilities and staff, and even mailing lists, to the point that its own personnel began to complain.

In making the deal with THEN, UCLA waived its legal remedies of preliminary and permanent injunction, agreed to secrecy about the deal through a confidentiality clause in the contract, and apparently seriously entertained no other bids for these services. UCLA also appears to have circumvented the review and oversight of the Academic Senate, including the standing committee on Extension, and risked allegations of conflict of interest. John Kobara, vice-chancellor of UCLA for marketing and public relations, became the president of THEN. There was at least one instance of preferential hiring when Arkatov's brother-in-law was given a job at UNEX, over the strenuous objections of the associate dean. Moreover, it appears that UCLA sidestepped Regental review of the contract in the final hours before it was signed; the University of California Board of Regents, in whose name the contract was signed, never even saw much less approved the unprecedented arrangement. Finally, in claiming rights to the intellectual property embodied in course materials authored by instructors, without ever having obtained an assignment of these rights, the parties appear to have violated copyright law and proceeded without any legal foundation.

Late in the summer of 1993, Lapiner and Ralph Ochoa, who was representing Arkatov, met with Chancellor Charles Young to discuss the proposed project. Afterward Lapiner wrote Young that the meeting had been of great value and predicted that "the time we spent with Ralph Ochoa will prove as profitable (in all senses of the word) for UCLA and UCLA Extension." Lapiner and his colleagues had great expectations. They noted that the financial opportunities "appear strongly to outweigh the risks. . . . The estimated revenue projections, based on the market research to date, would seem to provide resources greatly in excess of costs." While UNEX would bear initial costs, "the magnitude of the financial returns thereafter should provide Extension with the assurance that its 'venture capital' will have been well invested." They projected a gross distribution to UCLA by the second year of between three and four million dollars, which would "grow exponentially" thereafter, to an estimated thirty-one million in year four—"an amount comparable to our total annual revenue for all programs over the last few years." Thus, there was, in their view, a "compelling economic argument." "The persuasive reason to move forward . . . is that the spread between expenses and potential revenue is of such magnitude that even a significantly smaller profit [than projected] is still likely to be sizable."

As negotiations continued, the projections became more sober, as indicated in the evolving terms for termination of the agreement. At first UCLA had the right to terminate if there were no revenues after two years, or less than fifty million after five years, or one hundred million after seven years. This was later reduced drastically to less than three million after five years; when the contract was signed the figure was reduced further to two million after five years. Three years later, in the face of practical operational realities, the figure was finally dropped down to $400,000, more than a hundred-fold reduction from the original estimate of fifty million. And as the five-year deadline approached in 1999, the company, facing considerable losses and pleading poverty, was barely able to meet even that condition.

The original expectations of financial returns produced an eagerness on the part of UCLA that caused them to throw caution to the wind. This is clear in their agreement to waive legal safeguards of the public interest. In its proposed agreement, THEN, following the example of the entertainment industry, included a requirement that both UNEX and all participating instructors had to waive their legal rights to preliminary and injunctive relief in the event of any dispute. THEN would be willing to settle for monetary compensation but did not want to risk the interruption of its operations or the rescission of UNEX's assignment of rights to THEN, which an injunction would entail.

Thus they insisted that "under no circumstances shall the instructor [or UNEX] be entitled to injunctive relief."

The university's counsel viewed this request as out of the question. "For obvious reasons," Ruth Simon wrote to Arkatov's attorney, "we cannot agree to include this paragraph, or any part of it, in our contract with the instructor or THEN . . . any mention of limitation of remedies, whether by Instructor or by UNEX, will inflame the Regents. . . . We simply cannot agree to any limitation of our remedies." On the eve of the signing THEN continued to insist that the waiving of injunctive relief was "standard practice in the film, TV, publishing, and recording industry where producers/distributors are making huge investment in product." "No one," THEN insisted, "would want to give the right to injunctive relief to several hundred instructors." The Office of General Counsel and Chancellor Young both still maintained that such a limitation of their remedies was "unacceptable."

Aside from sound legal practice, there was a particular reason why UCLA was especially sensitive to THEN's request regarding limitation of remedies, which was indicated by Simon's warning that it would "inflame the Regents." At the very time the agreement with THEN was being negotiated a public scandal erupted regarding an earlier episode involving the junk-bond felon Michael Milken. Without the Regents' knowledge, UCLA, under the auspices of Young and Simon, had contracted with Milken for the delivery of some lectures and had agreed to grant Milken exclusive rights to the recordings. In addition, UCLA agreed to waive its right to injunctive relief. When the Regents belatedly found out about this contract, they were furious. Aside from their anger at having heard about it only after the fact, they were particularly upset about the assignment of exclusive rights and the limitation of remedies.

Regent Frank W. Clark, a prominent attorney, bemoaned the fact that "UCLA officials waived the university's right to rescind the agreement or even file an injunction against [Milken]." "There are serious legal problems with this document," he declared. Regent Ward Connerly went so far as to suggest that the Regents should take back the powers it delegates to university administrators to make deals. At the same time, two state senators harshly criticized UCLA for "waiving virtually all their legal rights" and suggested that UCLA officials "were seduced" by Milken's prior multimillion-dollar donations to the university.

Now confronted by THEN's request for a similar waiver of remedies, UCLA officials were understandably hesitant—until the final hour. In the end, after getting THEN to agree to particular conditions for termination—which included the establishment of a financial benchmark (two million by the fifth year), and the granting to UNEX of the specific rights to specify classes, update courses, and give final approval of course content—UCLA capitulated. Once again UCLA agreed (and without their knowledge or consent committed its instructors to agree) to waive its right to preliminary and permanent injunctive relief. UCLA agreed that there could be no termination of exploitation rights to the course recordings, just of production rights. (In the event of a termination of the production of new courses, THEN would continue to be able to market already existing recordings.) Three days before the signing of the deal, Simon informed THEN's lawyer of her conversation with Jim Holtz, general counsel of the University of California, who, she reported, was "comfortable with the way we negotiated the question of injunctive relief."

In the wake of the Milken imbroglio, the Board of Regents were most disturbed that they had only learned about the agreement belatedly, after it was too late to rescind or revise. For this reason, among others, UCLA officials were sensitive to the need to have the Regents sign off on the THEN deal. From the start, therefore, they insisted upon Regental approval. "The project being proposed by THEN is unique in its scope," UCLA general counsel Ruth Simon wrote to Arkatov's attorney in December 1993. "It is the sheer magnitude that raises complex questions. We will also need to be assured that the Regents is consulted about the use of its name in all forms of marketing and presentation in the videotapes."

UCLA's insistence upon securing the necessary high-level support and authorization from the chancellor and the Regents slowed down the negotiating process, to Arkatov's mounting dismay. Intent upon attracting investors and getting his show on the road, and habituated to the fast and loose deal making of the entertainment industry, Arkatov grew increasingly impatient and tried to pressure UCLA into moving more quickly. UCLA nevertheless maintained its position on the necessity of Regental approval. In February Lapiner's associate dean, Michael Bley, wrote to him that "Alan's [Arkatov] concern has increased about the university's ability to move with any speed, relative to normal industry standards, particularly with the specter looming of the necessity of Regental approval. Ralph [Ochoa] spoke with me as well as Alan noting that any activity without such a step, given the high visibility of the project, could possibly be quite detrimental." (Arkatov later recalled that Ochoa "made sure that we follow the necessary steps to secure approval from the Chancellor and Regents.") Bley went on to report that they "also discussed the possibility of effecting an interim compromise and 'conciliatory' measure of good faith on the part of the university, which would meet Alan's needs, by issuing a signed contract (with the Chancellor's approval) subject to Regental clearance. Ralph felt comfortable pursuing this possibility [with Chancellor Young]." "However," Bley cautioned, "conversations today with Ruth [Simon] indicated that such actions have not been well-received in the past."

The specter of Michael Milken clearly haunted the negotiations, in contradictory ways. On the one hand, the Regents' reaction to having heard about the Milken deal after the fact made UCLA officials sensitive to the need for prior Regental approval. On the other hand, the Regents' critical response to the granting of exclusive rights to Milken and the waiving of legal remedies made the officials extremely wary of having the Regents review a new deal that contained the very same provisions. In February 1994, Simon wrote a memorandum to her file about discussions with Lapiner and Arkatov, noting that "Robert presented the issues to Alan as political issues that needed to be resolved in order to get the deal through the Regents." A month later, after the Milken scandal hit the press, Arkatov expressed concern about the key issues of copyright assignment and the waiving of remedies. In response, Simon unsuccessfully proposed a new clause for the contract: "Approvals. THEN acknowledges that no agreement between the parties shall be effective unless and until approval by the UCOP [University of California Office of the President] and by the Regents at a meeting regularly noticed and held." Arkatov's attorney replied in a phone conversation that "approvals be changed to disapprovals," i.e. that the agreement would stand unless UCOP and the Regents disapproved within sixty days of the signing. By this novel construction the Regents, the supreme legal authority of the University of California, would be relegated to a mere rubber-stamp function, after the fact and within a limited time. Neither version of this clause survived the day. The controversy they reflected, however, persisted until the eleventh hour before the agreement was signed.

At the end of May, a month before the signing, Ruth Simon was still assuming that Regental approval was on the agenda. She wrote to an official at San Francisco State University for a copy of a contract between that institution and the Wadsworth Publishing Company, which Arkatov suggested might strengthen their case before the Regents. "My interest in this," Simon explained, "is that we are in the midst of negotiating a distance learning contract which will go before the Regents; our thought is that the SFSU agreement may be helpful as a point of comparison for the Regents." Two weeks later, however, after another meeting between Lapiner, Ralph Ochoa and Chancellor Young, she appears to have moved markedly in Arkatov's direction. Reporting on arrangements for a meeting between the UCLA chancellor and several vice presidents and the general counsel of the University of California Office of the President, Simon reminded Arkatov that "as you know, UCOP approval is critical to an item being placed on the Regents' agenda." She added without reservations, however, "Chancellor Young intends to raise with the vice presidents whether Robert [Lapiner] can sign the agreement before it is presented to the Regents, subject, of course, to the Regents' right to disapprove." Simon had now clearly endorsed Arkatov's position.

In the end the Regents were not even afforded the right of after-the-fact disapproval. According to Ann Shaw, the secretary of the Regents, the Regents never saw the agreement either before or after it was signed. Chancellor Young, after meeting with Ochoa and Lapiner and the University of California vice presidents and general counsel, unilaterally gave Lapiner permission to sign the deal. Arkatov acknowledged Young's role in a thank-you letter a few weeks after the signing. "I want to thank you for providing THEN the opportunity to create with UCLA Extension a new vision of distance learning for continuing education." Lapiner was more explicit. In a letter to Arkatov a year later he referred to "Chancellor Young's involvement in my intra-campus negotiations that allowed us to sign our contract." Thus, the Regents did not know about this new Milken-like undertaking, with its assignment of exclusive copyright to a private firm and its waiver of legal remedies. When Regent Ward Connerly was finally informed about the deal in 1999, by UCLA English professor Edward Condren, he expressed complete surprise. In all probability, had the Regents rightfully been given the opportunity to review the agreement between UCLA and THEN, as was anxiously anticipated throughout the negotiations, the deal would never have been approved.

If UCLA officials bent the rules of established procedure by doing an end run around the Regents, it appears they went even further in granting THEN exclusive electronic rights to all UNEX courses without the approval of the instructors: they broke the law. According to the US Copyright Act an author is automatically endowed with all rights (including electronic distribution rights) to his or her work—in this case the course material—unless some or all of those rights have been assigned in writing to another party (as a condition of employment or on a contract basis). It is abundantly clear from the documentary record that both UCLA and THEN were fully aware of this requirement from the start, namely, that they had to secure a written assignment from the instructors as a precondition of doing business, and that they chose ultimately to ignore it.

In the prospectus for his new company Arkatov had emphasized that "the owners of intellectual properties . . . will be the leaders and winner in the field" and in his "letter of intent" to Lapiner he made it explicit that he understood that the intellectual property in question belonged in part or entirely to the instructors. "Extension [UNEX] is in the business of employing individuals ('teachers') to prepare and provide the classes," he wrote to Lapiner. "Network [THEN] is desirous of acquiring the exclusive right to produce and exploit Programs based upon the classes" and would like to negotiate an agreement in which "Extension shall grant to Network the sole and exclusive right to exhibit and otherwise exploit such programs by all means and media now known or hereafter devised . . . throughout the world." In return for this grant of rights, UNEX would receive a proportion of the net profits and "Extension shall divide such net profit participation between Extension and the teachers." Although the teachers were not party to the negotiations, their compensated contribution was clearly seen as being essential to the enterprise.

From the earliest discussions about the proposed agreement within UNEX, questions were raised about the legal rights of the instructors and the legality of UNEX granting THEN, on the instructors' behalf, rights to their course materials. One of Lapiner's staff, Inju Sturgeon, noted that "since many courses and course materials are 'authored' by our instructors who receive a fairly modest salary in the context of our nonprofit status, I would anticipate some legal objections to our just 'selling' their work and course materials to a profit-making business enterprise." Fred Churchill, another UNEX staff member, also raised the "copyright issue of who owns the material—UNEX or the instructor." In the light of these concerns, Lapiner sought the advice of UCLA's experts on such matters.

In November 1993 Lapiner received a report from Connie Little of UCLA's Budget and Planning Office about her discussion of the matter with Carli Rodgers, UCLA's Copyright Officer. "During my discussion with Carli it became apparent that we must see the copyright wording in the contract with THEN due to several issues. The most important issue is even if we re-work the course material and have the course reapproved, all we own is the course material; the presentation is that of the instructor and is copyrightable to him/her." In essence, UCLA might perhaps own the physical course materials but not the copyright to the content, which belonged to the author/instructor. A few days after receiving this clarification, Lapiner reviewed a letter from Arkatov's attorney that maintained that THEN would own the copyright to the recordings of UNEX courses and he noted in the margin "we need permission of each instructor."

Arkatov's attorney clearly understood this as well and had already begun to draft an "instructor's contract" that would provide the legally required written assignment of rights. "Instructors and guest lecturers will enter into agreements directly with Extension," he wrote. "Each such agreement shall provide that THEN is an intended third party beneficiary and that the rights of the Instructors and guest lecturers in and to such courses are being assigned by Extension to THEN." "As between Extension and THEN," he added, "Extension shall be the sole party responsible for compensating such Instructors and guest lecturers for their services and for any rights they convey with respect to Extension courses being videotaped for THEN." Again, both parties to the proposed agreement understood fully that they had to secure a written assignment of rights from the Instructors as a legal precondition for their joint enterprise. The following month UCLA's general counsel wrote to Arkatov's attorney, "while Extension is willing to agree to exclusivity, we must together face the difficulty of getting the Instructors to agree."

In January 1994 Simon received confirmation of this understanding regarding "copyright ownership in lectures" and conveyed it to Arkatov's counsel. "I have consulted with the Office of the General Counsel [of the University of California] in Oakland about interpretation of the UC Policy on Copyright Ownership. I have been informed that it is most likely that the rights in a lecture would be determined under Section IV.A. of that policy, as 'scholarly/aesthetic work.' A lecture read from an outline or a prepared text would have a different status from one given extemporaneously, but under Section IV.A., the copyright to the outline or text would belong to the faculty member." "It seems, therefore," she once again concluded, "that in every case there will have to be an assignment of copyright to the Regents." Before UNEX, acting on behalf of the Regents, could make any grant of rights to THEN, it would itself first have to secure an assignment of those rights from the instructors.

The mechanism envisioned for this transfer of rights from the instructors to UNEX was the "instructor's agreement," initially a part of the text of the

UNEX–THEN agreement and later appended as an expanded "Exhibit A" at Simon's suggestion. "We think that the body of the Agreement should simply refer to UNEX's understanding to use its best efforts to have Instructors sign an agreement in the form of Exhibit A attached to the Agreement," she wrote to Arkatov's attorney. "We therefore suggest that the paragraph read simply: UNEX shall exert its reasonable best efforts to cause the Instructors to enter into agreements concerning the production and exploitation of the Recordings." Eager to embark upon what they imagined was a golden opportunity, UCLA officials had thus decided to contractually assume the burden of getting the instructors to sign on to the project by surrendering their copyright.

As Simon had anticipated, however, the task would prove "difficult." THEN's formulation of the "instructor agreement" declared that "instructor shall warrant, represent, and covenant that instructor: has the full right, power, and authority to enter into and perform the agreement and to grant to and vest in UNEX, for assignment to THEN, all rights therein set forth, free and clear of all claims, rights, and obligations whatsoever."[2] Upon first reading this language, Simon confided to Arkatov's attorney, "we do not think any Instructor would agree to this." Indeed, a preliminary survey of instructors about the proposed deal had already indicated precisely that. In June 1994, just weeks before the agreement was signed, a summary report of a meeting of the parties (excluding the instructors) indicated that they all understood that instructor cooperation would not be forthcoming. The view of the UC Office of General Counsel was summarized: "Must cut back on rights. Unlikely that Instructors will sign." The view of UNEX was: "Concerned that low-paid UNEX Instructors will not find compensation attractive enough to sign away rights."

The summary of THEN's position is startling: "THEN believes it needs to have all included rights. Willing to take risk that Instructors will not sign." Fully aware that instructors would more than likely not sign the instructors agreement, the acknowledged legal sine qua non for the deal, THEN decided to proceed anyway, and so too did UCLA. When asked by this author five years later why he signed the agreement in the knowledge that it lacked a secure legal foundation, Arkatov answered—sidestepping the question but not denying the truth of the allegation—"it was an exciting opportunity to play a significant role in helping to expand UNEX's outreach to the world via distance education."

---

2. This instructor agreement is discussed in greater detail in Chapter Three above.

For four years after the signing of the agreement, and after the effort shift-ed its focus from videotape reproductions to online delivery, UNEX again and again sought in vain to secure a written assignment of rights from the instruc-tors, without which it had no legal basis for its grant of rights to THEN. In the meantime, the partners earnestly embarked upon the profit-making business of delivering UNEX courses electronically anyway, with THEN (later renamed Onlinelearning.net) declaring to the world that it held "exclusive electronic rights" to all UNEX courses.

Throughout 1995, with the shift to online delivery, significant tensions emerged between the partners regarding the suitability of the existing agree-ment to the new situation. Lapiner argued in vain that they needed to negoti-ate a significantly amended contract while Arkatov maintained that all of the existing provisions applied equally to online delivery. One of the central ques-tions that arose was whether or not the instructors were being offered incen-tives adequate enough to cause them to surrender their copyright. At the same time, some UCLA officials, including Lapiner, began to entertain the wishful thinking that the Regents might automatically own the copyright in the online medium and that there would therefore be no need for an instructor assign-ment of rights to the university. Nevertheless, as obligated by the agreement, UNEX undertook to get the instructors to sign the instructor agreement. The effort was overseen by Kathleen McGuire who at the beginning of 1996 began to receive very clear signals from her staff about "instructor reticence," a resist-ance which had, if anything, increased with the shift to online delivery.

In February 1996 McGuire and Lapiner received a memo about the situa-tion from staff member Linda Venis. "We are currently planning our on-line curriculum," wrote Venis, "but do not want to enter these courses in the [cata-log]—commit to them for Summer—until we can determine whether the instructors will sign the contract. . . . We need to know now if we can count on our instructors." Venis was not optimistic. "It is important to stress that the response to signing the contract thus far, based on individual discussions and our own meeting with on-line instructors, is 'No.' I know that, Kathy, you reit-erated that instructors are 'only' signing away recording rights—fair enough in the context of video and audio, as those are akin to performances which can be recreated. However—and it is a huge 'however'—'recording rights' in the on-line context are quite different, as the lessons transmitted would be owned in perpetuity by THEN and could be used in any electronic format." "Electronic publishing is a huge issue with our instructors," Venis stressed, and she recommended sending copies of the instructor contract to all instructors as soon as possible to get a good reading. She suggested that UNEX hire an in-house legal consultant who could advise instructors about the contract, indicating that she and her staff were "very uncomfortable" interpreting it. In the end, and in no uncertain terms, she warned her superiors that "we anticipate that most, if not all, on-line instructors will not sign away the right to their materials" and emphasized that "a timeline and some real consideration about what happens if the instructors refuse to sign the on-line contract is critical."

The following week Lapiner wrote to Arkatov about "our instructors' refusal," again insisting on the inadequacy of the existing agreement in the online context. (A week later Lapiner was, according to his own account, compelled by Chancellor Young to sign an amendment that simply declared that the original agreement would apply to online delivery.) Especially in the new online environment, Lapiner reported, "no faculty member will surrender rights." With regard to "intellectual property rights," he noted, "most UNEX instructors and all UCLA faculty queried will not agree to assigning these to THEN in perpetuity, or probably at all." Echoing Venis, he stressed the fact that "this has become the critical impediment to realizing the agreement."

In March 1996, despite the fact that all parties acknowledged that there were as yet "no instructor contracts," the decision was made to begin online delivery of UNEX courses by THEN on a pilot basis during the spring term. As UNEX's new associate dean, David Menninger, rather matter-of-factly and cryptically reported that fateful step to Arkatov, "it was agreed that execution of instructor agreements would not be a requirement for courses to be offered in Spring 1996 on a pilot basis." He also indicated that UNEX was already preparing for a full online program with THEN for the summer. In anticipation of the summer program, UNEX redoubled its efforts to get the instructors to sign their contracts. "It was agreed that development and selection of courses for Summer is a priority, as is finalization of terms for a revised instructor's agreement," summarized Menninger at a senior staff meeting. McGuire noted in her notes of the meeting that "the model for the instructor contract needs to move fast, if [supervisors] are to contact instructors for summer courses." A week later Arkatov informed Menninger that "Dean Lapiner has asked us to focus on the instructor agreement as a top priority (a new draft has been sent to Kathy McGuire)."

Lapiner was intent upon making the partnership with THEN a success; reminding them of "the Chancellor's expectations," he urged his staff to do their "best to make this project a visibly important and successful enterprise." Likewise, McGuire exhorted the staff: "I am encouraging you to participate heartily in this venture by proposing more online courses." But all the while the instructor agreements were not forthcoming, either for the summer or even the fall terms. In the middle of the summer, McGuire informed course supervisors that "the status of the instructor contract is still liquid" and that, even given THEN's willingness to redraft the terms, "a final contract will probably not be available until August 26." By mid-August McGuire was now referring to "the infamous instructor contract" and internal UNEX communications took note of the "unresolved instructor contractual issues." Despite this difficulty, UNEX issued a press release announcing the pathbreaking collaborative venture with THEN, the success of the pilot courses, and robust plans for the fall. The agreement, UNEX explained, gives THEN "exclusive rights to electronic recordings of UNEX courses" in return for a percentage of revenues; moreover, UNEX attested, "the agreement . . . ensures that all intellectual property rights . . . are appropriately protected."

Within the university, apparently, not everyone was so sure, especially in the absence of any agreement with the instructors. At the end of December 1996, Lapiner wrote to UCLA vice chancellor John Kobara, due to become THEN's president in January. "As you probably know, in some noisy quarters within UCLA and UNEX itself, the contract was and continues to be attacked as 'selling' UCLA property, and out of synch with UC policy on ownership of intellectual property." Again, Lapiner urged THEN to provide UNEX with a revised instructor agreement suitable for online course delivery and acceptable to instructors. Internally, UNEX had already adopted a policy of giving instructors a one-time "honorarium" of five hundred dollars for course development, as an incentive to instructors and tacit compensation for the surrender of their intellectual property rights. At the same time, UNEX officials moved further in their wishful thinking that the university somehow already automatically owned these rights in the online context. Accordingly, Menninger began to contest THEN's public claims that it owned "exclusive electronic rights to UNEX courses" and suggested that THEN adopt more precise language that would convey the fact that it held the rights to online "distribution" of the courses but not to the "content," which, Menninger believed, were retained by the Regents.

By this time, early 1997, tension between UNEX and THEN was reaching the breaking point, as each party blamed the other for the slow start-up of operations; THEN accused UNEX of dragging its feet in the development of new online courses and disputing the nature and extent of THEN's acquired rights, while UNEX complained about THEN's failure to produce promised market research, cost reimbursements and royalties, and a "feasible instructor contract for online production." By mid-April, Arkatov's lawyer accused Lapiner, UNEX, UCLA, and the Regents of "material breach" and threatened to file suit. A week later, Menninger inquired of McGuire, "Kathy, just to confirm: we never settled the instructor's agreement, did we?" "No," McGuire replied, "it's just sort of sitting there . . . they [THEN] may have abandoned the idea."

A few weeks later—now nearly three years after the UNEX-THEN deal was signed—Menninger once again brought the matter of the instructor agreement up with THEN. "This brings back into focus the instructor agreement that has not yet been finalized," he wrote Kobara. "Ideally the agreement will have terms sufficient to cover any activity between UNEX and THEN, be it online or taped recording. If THEN has determined the terms that it believes need to be included in a satisfactory instructor agreement/ release, please forward them to me and I will work to get the process moving again toward mutual agreement." "Yes," Kobara replied, "we need to address the overall instructor agreement issue. It seems to me that we should start anew. What do you suggest as the next logical step in this process? Should we draft something? I need your advice on how to proceed to avoid whatever problems we encountered in the last go-around." The next day Menninger explained the situation to Kobara. "Regarding the instructor agreement; with the switch in emphasis to online a year ago, the draft agreement attached to the UNEX/THEN contract became problematic. (There had already been indications in any case of instructor resistance to the terms of the agreement anyway.) THEN agreed to the need to revise the agreement to make it more acceptable and relevant to online, and was to have provided UNEX with a starting position to negotiate into a final agreement that UNEX would then present to instructors for execution. That's still where we need to pick things up. So, yes, a draft of your preferred terms are the place to start."

Plainly, at least up to this point officials of UNEX and UCLA were still insistent upon the need for a written assignment of rights from the instructors, even with the shift to online course delivery and even while some of them had begun to imagine that the university could automatically claim these rights without it. In her response to the breach of contract charge levelled by THEN's attorney, UCLA general counsel Simon blamed THEN for the "uneven progress" in the online area, the lack of revenues to "UNEX and its instructors" and, in particular, for "the absence of an instructor's agreement." "THEN has not followed through on this with a clear statement of its expectations for such an agreement and a prompt negotiation of final terms." "A workable instructor contract that spells out to instructors what their rights are," Simon emphasized, "is the foundation of a solid working relationship with UNEX instructors and UCLA faculty."

In January 1998, the public controversy erupted over the UNEX-THEN deal. By this time UNEX officials had somehow firmly convinced themselves that an instructors agreement was no longer necessary and that the Regents could claim rights to course material absent any such assignment. In response to public questions raised about intellectual property rights, Lapiner wrote to the new UCLA chancellor, Albert Carnesale, and Julie Gordon of the UC Office of the President that "all intellectual property rights to materials and curricula belong to the instructor and the Regents." In his disarmingly simple assertion Lapiner of course begged the crucial question as to the distinction between, and the legal relationship between, the instructor and the Regents: how can the Regents claim author rights without author assignment? In response to this author's request for a copy of the UNEX-THEN contract, including the instructor's agreement, Menninger took the next step, explaining that "since the focus of the Extension/THEN relationship has shifted to Extension online courses, for which the Regents of the UC retain ownership, no such instructor agreement has ever been used, nor is any further need anticipated." Like magic, through the devices of determined self-delusion and rhetorical legerdemain, the heretofore acknowledged legal foundation of the entire deal had been rendered irrelevant.

Of course, it was not at all irrelevant, as other universities that had begun parallel online efforts well understood. Thus even UNEX's major rival within the University of California system, the extension program of UC Berkeley (which had its own deal with America Online), required its online instructors to sign an instructor agreement, assigning copyright to the Regents, as a condition of employment. UCLA, however, had chosen to fly without wings. In May 1998, Jeff Gerdes, a UCLA economics instructor, inquired about the UNEX program and requested clarification of its intellectual property policy. Kathy McGuire responded with an extended explanation based upon an amended agreement not made public until July 1999. According to this amended contract, she assured Gerdes, the rights granted to THEN (recently renamed Onlinelearning.net) were "limited to marketing and distribution during the term of the contract" and copyright ownership was retained by the author. "Extension policy on ownership of course materials conforms to standard university policy," she explained. "Faculty and instructors own materials they develop, whatever the medium of instruction." The concern over copyright was thus dismissed as a non-issue. "It's not an issue, period," a UNEX associate dean declared to the *San Francisco Chronicle.* "Nobody has pointed to anybody who's ever had to sign over their rights."

But that was precisely the issue. There never was any assignment of rights by the author. As McGuire maintained, the faculty and instructors retained ownership of the copyright to the materials they developed. How, then, did THEN (Onlinelearning.net) obtain the now "limited" commercial rights of marketing and distribution of the materials? Ownership of copyright entails the ownership of all rights to the author's creation, including the commercially crucial ones of marketing and distribution. According to the Copyright Act, in the absence of a written assignment of those specified rights by the author directly or indirectly to THEN, via assignment to the Regents, the company would have no rights whatsoever with which to conduct business.

The second amendment to the UNEX-THEN agreement, signed by Lapiner and Kobara on July 8, 1999, but effective January 1, 1998, indelibly enshrined the slippery and self-contradictory thinking of the parties. It asserted that the instructors and the Regents retained ownership of the copyright while failing either to clarify the precise nature of the relationship between instructors and the Regents or to account for the possession of rights by the Regents (and, hence, the granting of rights by the Regents to Onlinelearning.net) in the absence of any assignment by the author-instructor, as required by law. Whereas in her explanation of the copyright policy to Gerdes, presumably based upon this amendment, McGuire had forthrightly stated that the faculty and instructors owned the materials they developed, in the actual amendment the matter was fudged. In the critical clauses the amendment alternately coupled the instructors with the Regents and UNEX when spelling out the ownership of rights. "As between OLN, on the one hand, and the Regents and the Instructors, on the other hand, the Regents or the Instructors, as appropriate, shall be the owner of all right, title and interest, including without limitation, the copyright, in and to all content, class material and curricula (collectively the 'Course Materials') of UNEX Classes produced by or for OLN hereunder, and, for purposes of Title 17 of the US Code, also known as the Copyright Act of 1976, as amended (the 'Copyright Act') UNEX and the Instructors shall be deemed the author of the Course Materials." There is no provision for any assignment from the instructor to UNEX or the Regents, merely the simple assertion of authorship and ownership by UNEX and the Regents.

Moreover, according to the amendment, all of these rights presumably held by the instructors, the Regents, and UNEX were now restricted, "subject to the exclusive right to distribute UNEX's Classes by On-Line Means conveyed to OLN herein." Since the amendment was signed by Lapiner, on behalf of UNEX and the Regents, and the instructors were neither party to the negotiations nor signatories of the amendment, it is clear that the exclusive distribution rights granted OLN were being conveyed by UNEX and the Regents without any instructor assignment to UNEX, the Regents, or OLN. Again, if the instructor was the author and owner of "all right," as the amendment declares, how did OLN obtain its right of distribution absent instructor assignment? If, as the parties claim, OLN was granted its rights by the Regents and UNEX, how did the Regents and UNEX obtain them in the first place, absent the instructor assignment that both signatories to the amendment had long known (and presumably still knew) was legally required? (In November 1998, this author had an opportunity to discuss the matter with both Lapiner and Kobara at a joint UNEX-OLN event. Lapiner insisted that the amendment solved the copyright problem and pointed out that, as indicated in the amendment, instructors would be given "full knowledge" of the UNEX-OLN arrangement and their attendant responsibilities. I maintained that any agreement between the two signatories, whatever the specific language regarding instructors, was insufficient without a written assignment from the instructors themselves. Kobara nodded, turned to Lapiner and said, "He's right.") For all the inventiveness and effort of the parties, the collaboration between UNEX and OLN, it appears, remained illegal.

One person who has most forcefully questioned the legality of the arrangement is Edward Condren, a longtime UCLA English professor and Chaucer scholar who for many years has moonlighted as a copyright expert in legal cases involving the entertainment industry. He sat on one of the Academic Senate committees that had been circumvented by the UNEX-THEN entrepreneurs in their rush to cement the deal and later had an opportunity to question Lapiner during a belated committee inquiry. He does not see how the instructors can own the copyright, on the one hand, and OLN have exclusive distribution rights, on the other; both cannot be true without some written assignment from the instructor to OLN. In Condren's informed view, what the amendment "practically means is that I may own the house, but you have the right to rent it to somebody and get revenue from it. In other words, it is absurd. Federal law makes it abundantly clear that the ownership of copyright means the right to market, distribute, and so forth." Condren's legal opinion appears sound in light of the law but it is no substitute for the opinion of a court, which alone could declare the arrangement illegal.

Condren believes that, if not challenged (or corrected voluntarily), the arrangement could set a dangerous precedent for faculty. Over time the arrange-ment could someday be sanctioned by a court as accepted or established prac-tice and faculty would forfeit copyright to the university by default. And the loss of their intellectual property rights to their course materials, he argues, would invariably lead to the loss of their academic freedom as well, in that "it would undermine the legal protection that enables faculty to freely express their views without fear of censorship or appropriation of their ideas." But where might such a challenge come from? What financially strapped non-unionized online instructor who must depend upon the good graces of administrators for the next job and paycheck would be willing to file an infringement suit? And what member of the California population would be so motivated to file fraud charges against OLN, especially given the financial and legal resources at its disposal? In the summer of 1994, on the eve of the signing of the UNEX-THEN agreement, THEN indicated its willingness to take the risk of proceeding with its proposed project knowing that instructors might not sign over their rights. So far it appears to have been a risk worth taking.

As a cautionary tale in the commodification of higher education, this account of an early episode in the evolution of online distance education should give us pause. For, as the tale demonstrates, the glitter of gold drives men if not mad at least dangerously incautious. In an exchange with a UCLA vice chancellor, Ed Condren asked him what he thought might be done about the controversial arrangement and the administrator replied, "Ed, we are learning." So, in this spirit, let us learn from this example.

In large measure, the ethical and legal lapses evident in this enterprise resulted from a woeful lack of disclosure, debate, and democratic decision making. The existence of the arrangement, much less the details, was not even known by people at UCLA until the contract was made public by a visiting scholar from Canada four years after it was launched. And once it became known, and controversial, faculty were reluctant to talk about it for fear of administration reprisal. Silence, after all, is the unspoken but well-understood rule on campus, where collegial conformity and resigned cynicism pass for sophistication.

Meanwhile, administrators had anxieties of their own. Condren recalled that when his Academic Senate committee expressed an interest in participating in the negotiation of the second amendment, Lapiner exclaimed, "Arkatov will sue us!" (A not unreasonable expectation given the fact that Arkatov had twice threatened litigation against UNEX.) The entire enterprise, then, remains hermetically sealed from serious scrutiny: those outside the select circle of decision makers know little or nothing about what is happening, while those in the know are not talking. (Indeed, they are signing contracts that specifically prohibit them from talking.) Fuelled by technological and financial fantasies and given to entrepreneurial excess in imitation of their "real-world" role models, they are accountable to no one. Entrusted as they are with the stewardship of public institutions, their failings have dire consequences not only for themselves and their institutions but, more importantly, for the public that supports and relies upon the integrity of these institutions.

It is inconceivable that these administrative misjudgments would have prevailed had there been wider knowledge and discussion of the Arkatov initiative from the outset. Thus, one modest proposal would be an insistence upon full and timely disclosure and a required transparency of all transactions involving public goods and the public interest. All contracts above a specified dollar amount should as a matter of course be posted on the university website. And through the medium of open debate, wherein significant proposals are made subject to sober and dispassionate analysis, administrators should be encouraged to temper their enthusiasms and extravagant fantasies by bearing the burden of defending their decisions before they are taken. Above all, a new fashion must somehow be fostered of ongoing vigilance against such untoward and heretofore unchecked tendencies as have been described.

Finally, lest it be said that this episode is a particularly egregious example, the exception rather than the rule from which little can be generalized, it must be pointed out that, in retrospect, there is something almost quaint about the UCLA experience; if anything, things have gotten worse. At least UCLA administrators still sought revenues through the generation of fees paid for courses by students, and thus were required to develop courses, secure enrollments, and attend to the details of educational administration. The latest fashion among university administrators is to dispense with such drudgery and instead seek imagined fortunes through outright Wall Street speculation in the education industry. One university after another is either setting up its own for-profit online subsidiary or otherwise working with Street-wise collaborators to trade on its brand name in soliciting investors, enlarging its portfolio of stock options, and closing in on the IPO (initial public offering) jackpot. In the continuing gold rush of distance education, then, the aspirants from UCLA were, if anything, just beginners.

And now, in the year 2001, these latest academic entrepreneurs of distance education have begun to encounter the same sobering reality earlier confronted by UCLA and THEN, namely, that all that glitters is not gold. Columbia University's high-profile, for-profit venture Fathom is reported to be "having difficulty attracting both customers and outside investors," compelling the institution to put up an additional $10 million—on top of its original investment of $18.7 million—just to keep the thing afloat. According to Sarah Carr's report in the *Chronicle of Higher Education*, Columbia's administrators remain behind the venture whether or not it makes money.

However much it might enable administrators to restructure the institutions of higher education to their advantage vis-à-vis the professoriate, the investment in online education is no guarantee of increased revenues. "Reality is setting in among many distance education administrators," Carr reports. "They are realizing that putting programs online doesn't necessarily bring riches." Ironically, among those now preaching this new-found wisdom is none other than John Kobara, the UCLA vice chancellor who left the university to run Arkatov's company, which was founded upon the expectation of such riches. "The expectations were that online courses would be a new revenue source and something that colleges had to look into," Kobara remembered. "Today," he told Carr, "[chancellors and presidents] are going back and asking some important and tough questions, such as: 'Are we making any money off of it?' 'Can we even pay for it?' 'Have we estimated the full costs?'" Barely eight years after Lapiner and his UCLA colleagues first caught the fool's gold fever, Kobara mused aloud, "I don't think anybody has wild notions that it is going to be the most important revenue source."

6

Calling In the Cavalry:
Defense Dollars and the Future of Higher Education

I n the four years since the appearance of the first of the pieces now included in this book, nearly all post-secondary institutions have climbed aboard the distance education bandwagon in search of new revenues and in fear for their piece of higher education turf, only to discover the hard way the harsh realities of their enterprise. At the same time, however, in league with their private-sector partners, they have successfully sought and secured taxpayer subsidy of their online efforts, thereby partially offsetting their losses and the absence of any real market demand. In addition, university administrators have learned that the technology of online education, whether cost effective or not, has afforded them a relatively disarming way to restructure their institutions to their managerial advantage. Meanwhile, faculty resistance to this restructuring, and to the deprofessionalization of the professoriate that it entails, has increased and gained coherence and confidence.

As more colleges and universities have moved squarely into the realm of commercial online education, alone or in collaboration with private-sector partners, the distinction between non-profit and for-profit institutions has been blurred to the vanishing point. Not so very long ago, the post-secondary establishment railed against their for-profit online counterparts (in particular the University of Phoenix and Jones International), in defense of their own monopoly of higher education. The major trade associations like the American Council on Education and the American Association of Universities indignantly opposed formal accreditation of the pariah "for-profits" and lobbied virtuously against any relaxation of federal requirements for student aid that might support their "virtual" rivals. Today, these same organizations are striving to keep up with the Joneses. Joining forces with their erstwhile adversaries, they now rail against any and all state regulations that might cramp their own for-profit propensities, especially by limiting their part-time and distance-education offerings. In particular, they now vigorously oppose federal requirements for student aid eligibility—such as the "twelve-hour rule" defining the minimum full-time course load and the "50 percent rule" restricting institutions from offering more than half their courses at a distance—which were intended to safeguard public support of quality education against the fraud of diploma mills. In essence, universities are disconcertingly departing from academic tradition. Not only are they setting up their distinctly for-profit subsidiaries, like Columbia's Fathom or New York University's NYU Online. They are fast becoming de facto unabashed "for-profits" themselves, and doing so with abandon.

The academic rush to commercial enterprise has been a rocky ride for most institutions, however, especially in the wake of the dot-com collapse. The unanticipated costs associated with the development of online capability combined with an unstable and uncertain, and highly competitive, market belatedly gave even the most ardent enthusiasts pause. "Reality is setting in among many distance education administrators," reported the *Chronicle of Higher Education.* "They are realizing that putting programs online doesn't necessarily bring riches." Accordingly, now "distance education leaders predict that some administrators will slow or stop their expansion into online learning." Even the vanguard of private-sector online-education companies, whose siren song seduced many an administrator, felt the squeeze and cut back. E College laid off thirty-five of its employees, UNEXT eliminated fifty-two people, and Onlinelearning.net reportedly trimmed a third of its staff. What industry analyst Trace Urdan of E. R. Hambrecht and Company said about UNEXT could be said about them all: puffed up by IPO-dreaming investors, they are now "dealing with the realities of the private market."

Facing a fickle future, the intrepid entrepreneurs of online education turned in time-honored fashion to the taxpayer to bail them out. In addition to lobbying for indirect public subsidy through federal student aid, they have also become direct beneficiaries of taxpayer largesse through the Education Department's expanded Learning Anytime Anywhere Partnerships, which they lobbied vigorously both to create and enlarge. Most importantly, however, these strident capitalists have done what so many of their forebears have done before them when they found themselves in trouble: they have called in the cavalry.

After several years of lobbying by vendors and universities, and their trade associations like Educom/cause and the American Academy of Distance

Education and Training, the Clinton-Gore White House, by means of its Advanced Distributed Learning Initiative, secured the cooperation of the Department of Defense in artificially creating a market for these champions of free enterprise, at taxpayer expense. Announced first by the Army, in August 2000, and then followed up by the Navy and Air Force, the combined armed services decided to dedicate almost a billion dollars over five years to provide taxpayer-subsidized university-based distance education for active-duty personnel (and eventually their families as well). Overnight, the Department of Defense became the largest consumer of distance education in the land. The pioneers of online education had at last found their missing market.

The story is familiar. Throughout the history of industrial capitalism the military has served as midwife and handmaiden to private enterprise, supplying taxpayer support for technical innovation and thereafter providing a taxpayer-created market for new processes and products. The Army did it early on with interchangeable parts manufacture for muskets, which became the model for the so-called American system of manufactures. The Navy did it with the revolution in shipping and longshoring called "containerization." And the Air Force did it with the automation of metalworking by means of "numerical control," starting in the aerospace industry, which gave rise to computer-based batch-process manufacturing.

These epochal military-sponsored developments produced a radical restructuring of these industries, not only in terms of industrial process and product design and manufacture, but also in terms of labor relations, signaling the deskilling and ultimate demise of gunsmiths, dockworkers, and machinists. Together the armed services—the leading training organizations in the world and the primary source of nearly all instructional technologies of the last half century—are now undertaking to underwrite a similarly radical restructuring of the higher education industry, at the expense of the professoriate.

In August 2000, the Department of Defense sponsored an industry conference to kick off the new military distance-education initiative, get feedback from key industry players, and give the same players an opportunity to position themselves at the public trough. Over a thousand vendors, administrators, and military personnel were invited, but no students or faculty, whose exclusion followed a pattern established earlier with gunsmiths, dockworkers, and machinists. Speakers at the conference hailed from Educause and UNEXT rather than from the arts and sciences.

Later that month the Army revealed its six-hundred-million-dollar distance-education initiative. Citing free distance education as an incentive for
recruitment and reenlistment, the Army announced plans to issue a primary
contract with a private-sector "integrator" and subcontracts with other private vendors, colleges, and universities, whose staffs, in the wake of the industry conference, were no doubt already at work on proposals for a piece of the
action. "The Army will become the largest broker and customer of distance
learning in the United States.," the *Chronicle of Higher Education* noted,
describing the Army program as a "bonanza for colleges looking to either create or expand online offerings," a bold initiative that "could reassure college
administrators venturing into distance learning." "This is very concrete,"
Secretary of the Army Louis Caldera declared. "If you are trying to develop
this type of program, you can now go to your own president and say, 'Look,
there is a huge market out there.'" In January 2001, the Army announced the
successful bidders for the Army University Access Online contracts. The
accounting powerhouse Price Waterhouse Coopers was selected to be the
program "integrator," having won out in the competition with IBM, Arthur
Andersen, and Electronic Data Systems. The initial roster of the program
team included ten private firms and twenty-nine colleges, and other participants would be added later. Corporate partners included Blackboard,
Compaq, Fiberlink, Intel Online Services, and PeopleSoft. Academic partners
included Florida State University, Indiana University, Kansas State University,
Penn State, SUNY Empire State College, the University of Washington, Utah
State University, and the University of Massachusetts. "This is the largest e-
learning program of its kind," bellowed Michael Sousa, director of Price
Waterhouse Coopers' worldwide corporate training program. Judging from
the effects of similar military programs upon other industries, the
Department of Defense distance-education program is intended to have and
is bound to have far-reaching consequences for higher education. Distance-
education enthusiast Bob Kerrey, former senator and now New School
University president, explained the potential significance of the program.
"Not only is this a forward-looking investment, but an investment that will
have an impact on everything that is going on in all of our educational communities." As the *Chronicle of Higher Education* observed, the program "will
likely spur the development of new methods and technologies to provide distance learning and online courses at every level of education"; in the process,
"it will create a new kind of model for delivering education."

And just what kind of model might that be? Again, judging from earlier military experience in other industries, it is most likely to entail the familiar patterns of command, control, and precisely specified performance, in accordance with the hallmark military procurement principles of uniformity, standardization, modularization, capital-intensivity, system compatibility, interchangeability, measurability, and accountability—in short, a model of education as a machine, with standardized products and prescribed processes. The influence of such extra-academic military criteria on higher education is bound to reinforce and extend further already accelerating extra-academic commercial tendencies toward training and deprofessionalization.

The US military has long been the world's leader in on-the-job training and has, over the last century, developed and perfected a vast array of training techniques and technologies, many of which have subsequently been adopted by the civilian education system. The goal is the efficient training of precision-skilled personnel prepared to do a predetermined job according to specifications whenever and wherever necessary. The military (and now corporate) training slogan "just-in-time education," which derives from the famous Japanese system of inventory control, says it all: skilled personnel or, more precisely, the disembodied skills themselves (the person, presumably the focus of education, drops out of the picture) are viewed as inventory items in organizational planning. The military training regime is designed and refined to produce this product, in the shortest amount of time, with the least resources, and to the greatest effect. This is the model of education that will now be imposed upon higher education via the Department of Defense distance-education program.

According to Diane Stoskopf, director of the Army Continuing Education System, the specifications for university involvement in the military distance-education program "will be very detailed." Course content, curricula, and teaching methods, transparent in online format, will all be subject to military prescription, monitoring, and review and, hence, to implicit ideological censorship and a routinized abridgement of academic freedom—the customer, after all, is always right. All of the elements of instruction will be standardized and rendered interchangeable (through modularized "reusable content objects") in order to eliminate error and redundancy among subcontractors and guarantee quality control. "Getting schools to standardize their way of doing business is going to be a major obstacle," Stoskopf acknowledged. That such military standardization might entail an abandonment or relaxation of academic standards is also readily acknowledged. "Colleges in the Army program may also find themselves pushing against traditional academic boundaries to make the distance education program work," Stoskopf noted, such as giving academic credit in "non-traditional forms."

If the military distance-education program tilts toward a university-sanctioned regimen of skills training at the expense of academic norms and educational quality, it also accelerates the move toward the automation and deprofessionalization of university instruction and constitutes yet another threat to the very occupation of the professoriate. The first casualties of the program will be the military's own in-house training staff, whose work will be outsourced via the Internet to the universities. But university staff will surely pay a price as well. As the military, in collaboration with the university administration, underwrites an expansion of university online infrastructure and dictates the form and content of course development and delivery, faculty will face further abridgement of their academic freedom and autonomy, greater managerial supervision and discipline, a degradation of their working conditions and a deskilling of their work, the elimination of "redundant" courses, an appropriation of their intellectual property rights, a weakening of their collective bargaining power, and, ultimately, a reduction in their numbers. In short, the military presence will magnify, at taxpayer expense, the untoward impact that commercialized distance education is already having on institutions of higher education.

Whether financially remunerative or not—and with enough direct and indirect taxpayer subsidies who's to know or care?—the development of online education is nevertheless enabling administrators to restructure their institutions and labor relations to their managerial advantage, at faculty expense. At the heart of this transformation is the Taylorization of instructional labor, in which the teaching function is broken down into discrete components and assigned to different detail workers, a process described by Adam Smith and Charles Babbage at the dawn of the industrial revolution and perfected by Frederick Taylor, the father of so-called scientific management. This transformation is well underway in academia. At NYU Online, for example, which considers itself in the vanguard of institutional change, the job of instruction is assigned to a team of designated specialists in course design, development, content, delivery, and distribution. Where once a single professor would perform all of these tasks as an integrated whole, the detail workers now do only their part, with far less control over the process and substantially less pay—precisely the pattern established long ago with the shift from craft to industrial labor that culminated in the assembly worker of modern industry. As Bill Scheuerman, president of the New York State United University Professions, accurately described what is happening from the viewpoint of the faculty, it amounts to nothing less than the "disassembling and deskilling of the profession."

The deskilled job description that emerges from this process of deprofessionalization will no doubt become the template for future generations of academic labor. "I think the whole concept of adjunct profesorship is going to be very important," predicts NYU Online's CEO Gordon Macomber. Indeed, in the wake of this transformation of higher education thus far, we already witness the appearance of a new archetypal university instructor, one perfectly suited to the investor-imagined "university of the future." With wonder and excitement the *Chronicle of Higher Education* heralds the advent of a "new type of professor," namely, the "rapidly emerging type of distance education faculty member." This latest incarnation of university instructor hails not from academia but from the "corporate world." For this new breed, hired more for their "business savvy than their degree," "a focus on the bottom line is normal; tenure isn't." Says one such distance educator, "I love not only the teaching but the selling of it."

In this decidedly commercial ethos of distance education, administrators are predictably trying to win the cooperation of faculty by offering them a piece of the action. This is the latest strategy for getting the faculty to give up their intellectual property rights to course materials. Several high-profile "experiments" are underway, at North Texas University and Stevens Institute, for example. At both institutions, faculty are now given the incentive of royalty payments for the use of their course materials by the university as well as a part of the revenues from the licensing of these materials to other institutions. And, indeed, a good number of shortsighted faculty are trading their ownership and control for a fatter pay envelope, and even boasting about it. But the last laugh may not be theirs. At Stevens, for example, faculty may take their course materials with them if and when they leave only if they pay Stevens a licensing fee. More important, fixated on their own bottom line, they have lost sight of the larger picture of the deprofessionalization of the faculty, to which they are wittingly or unwittingly contributing through their actions, and they have failed to understand that the point of retaining professional ownership and control over the content of courses is not the enrichment of the professoriate but the preservation of quality higher education.

Of course not everyone is buying the new model of higher education. According to a *Chronicle of Higher Education* report, a recent Pentagon appropriation bill that includes some funding for distance education stipulates that the Army must continue using traditional classroom instruction in a training program for students at historically black colleges and universities rather than the distance education preferred by the Army. Apparently some members of Congress representing the interests of black constituents view distance education as a degraded, less valuable, form of education and have insisted that their constituents receive the genuine article instead. According to some a "digital divide" separates the haves from the have-nots in that only the privileged have access to computer technology, further disadvantaging the less privileged. In the case of distance education, however, the digital divide is turned on its head, with the have-nots being compelled to take their courses online while the haves get to do it in person. The dissenting clause in the appropriation bill is evidence that at least some are beginning to catch on to this reality and defy it.

At the other end of the socioeconomic spectrum, meanwhile, some of the elite have come to understand as well that distance education represents but a shadow of a genuine education. In 2001 MIT announced that it is planning to put all of its course material on websites for free Internet distribution. Of course MIT enjoys a secure market niche and plenty of funding, which affords it a degree of freedom unknown to most universities and enables it therefore to avoid some of the competitive compulsions of the higher education community. But the decision also reflects an understanding that students pay close to $40,000 a year to enroll at MIT for more than course materials. Of course, there are the benefits of a coveted degree and career-making connections, but there is also the quality education that comes from direct contact with fine teachers. As one promoter of the website distribution idea, civil engineering professor Steven Lerman, explained, "the syllabus and lecture notes are not an education, the education is what you do with the materials." No MIT bachelor's degree is offered online.

Such skepticism about distance education on the part of both the elite and the socially disadvantaged reflects a growing sophistication about what exactly is at stake here. Another sign is the growing struggle over the future of higher education, the context in which these *Digital Diploma Mills* articles were framed, and, in particular, the increasing and maturing resistance on the part of faculty organizations. A critical moment in this evolution was reached at roughly the same time the Department of Defense launched its distance-education initiative. At the end of August 2000, a potentially historic meeting was held at the Carnegie Institution in Washington. The meeting was called by the National Coalition for Universities in the Public Interest, an advocacy organization founded in 1983 by the author, Leonard Minsky, Ralph Nader, and others to fight against the corporatization of higher education. It brought together the leaders of the most progressive faculty unions in the United States and Canada. In attendance were representatives from the California Faculty Association, the union of the Cal State system and the largest higher education affiliate of the National Education Association; the United University Professions, the union of the SUNY system and the largest higher education affiliate of the American Federation of Teachers; the Professional Staff Congress, the union of the CUNY system, the largest urban university system in the United States; the American Association of University Professors; and the Canadian Association of University Teachers, the umbrella federation of faculty associations in Canada. The purpose of the meeting was to explore the possibility of establishing a common agency and strategy to fight against the commercial hijacking of public higher education and the entrenchment of a new "intellectual property regime" in academia.

Faculty organizations are becoming ever more alert to the fact that seemingly benign, progressive, and "technology-driven" administration distance-education initiatives may constitute a threat to faculty autonomy, intellectual property, and job security. At the same time, they are recognizing that faculty represent the last line of defense against the wholesale commercialization of academia, of which the commodification of instruction is just the latest manifestation, and that their fight is of a piece with the larger effort to preserve and enhance public higher education. They are fighting back, therefore, in myriad ways and on both local and national levels. The Washington meeting signalled a crystallization and potential consolidation of these struggles, and focused not upon this or that particular battle but upon the entire regime of intellectual property itself as inimical to the culture of academia. Decades after academia divested itself of classified research on behalf of the national security state on the grounds that such practice was in conflict with the free and open exchange of ideas to which university culture is dedicated, the academy has adopted practices on behalf of private corporations that have the very same corrosive consequences.

Participants expressed their concerns about the conversion of intellectual activity into commodity form for commercial sale, by means of patents, copyright, and licenses on these; about the resulting incremental enclosure of the "knowledge commons," through an array of proprietary arrangements, into a patchwork of private monopolies; about how universities have been adopting the corporate model of operation and outlook as they lock themselves into the corporate embrace, at the sacrifice of the core values of the academy; about the erosion of university culture as campuses have become a closed world of secret deals, non-disclosure agreements, prepublication reviews— the ensemble of practices that define the intellectual property regime; and about the campus atmosphere of silence, intimidation, and self-censorship that attends these arrangements and signals the demise of free speech and academic freedom.

Participants noted that these fundamental changes in higher education were the work of a relative handful of cynical and self-seeking, but otherwise perhaps well-intentioned, administrators who in reality constitute a distinct minority in academia, as compared with faculty, students, and the taxpaying public who support institutions of higher education. The participants resolved to try to reaffirm those ideals, to strive to recapture the ideological, rhetorical, and political initiative and moral high ground in the debates about higher education in order to reinvigorate a non-commercial conception of higher education and reconsecrate the intrinsic rather than mere utility value of universities. On behalf of those who truly embody education, teachers and students, as well as the larger community that education is meant to serve in a democratic society, the participants determined to reclaim this precious and unique social space as a realm of freedom, of open access, debate, inquiry, and learning—a place, in short, where the habits and highest ideals of democracy are a way of life. This, in essence, is the challenge before us. It's a tall order, to be sure, but it usually is.

Afterword

After September 11

I n the first article in this series (Chapter Two of this volume) I noted that online delivery of university courses rendered all course content and communication transparent to parties beyond the direct participants, in violation of the privileged relationship between teachers and students. I pointed out, for example that web-based courses at UCLA, the first major university to mandate websites for all its liberal arts courses, were routinely audited by the administration and that websites were typically created and updated by a cadre of administration-appointed technicians rather than by the instructors themselves; that UCLA's partner in online delivery, the Home Education Network (later Onlinelearning.net) regularly monitored their online offerings; that distance-education administrators at the University of Colorado were able to oversee their courses in progress as readily as if they were sitting at the back of the classroom; that, according to its designer, Marvin Goldberg, the popular WEB-CT courseware platform allowed for "lurking" by third parties as well as the automatic storage and retrieval of all online activities; and that the Virtual U courseware platform designed at Simon Fraser University automatically collected usage data, and conference transcript data (from chat rooms and other e-mail communications) for the use of systems developers. In light of such transparency, I asked readers to consider "what third parties will have access to [course] communications?"

At the time I was concerned about surreptitious administrative and commercial monitoring of students and instructors, as an invasion of privacy and mechanism for evaluation, intimidation, and the appropriation of intellectual property. But recent events have given new meaning and urgency to this question about online spying practices and capabilities. In the aftermath of September 11, governments have vastly enlarged their powers of surveillance, and surveillance of electronic communication in particular. Moreover, as we have seen, the US military itself has now become the single largest consumer of university-based online instruction.

With or without university administration compliance, government agencies are able as never before to monitor, access, and subpoena university course content and communications for alleged security purposes. The past record of university administrators in protecting faculty against such government actions is less than encouraging, as Cold War experience suggests.[1] Indeed, even before the attacks on the World Trade Center, the content and syllabi of courses offered by professors of the State University of New York (SUNY) system had become subject to political review by the Board of Trustees. Recent disclosures indicate that the University of Toronto has been the site of administration-sanctioned spying on faculty by Canada's CIA, the CSIS. At my own university, documents have just surfaced showing that the current vice president (academic) compiled lists of faculty participating in demonstrations during a legal strike.

Since September 11 such threats to academic freedom and free speech have multiplied dramatically. At California State University at Fresno a dean provided the Air Force with a list of foreign students without their knowledge or consent; at UCLA a librarian who had sent a critical e-mail response to a colleague's political message was summarily suspended; at the University of New Mexico, a professor who made an off-hand remark to students in his class about the September 11 attacks has been vilified by state legislators and his own administration and charged with unprofessional conduct; at California State University in Chico, a faculty member was deluged with hate mail for posting questions about US foreign policy; at the City University of New York, participants in a teach-in sponsored by the Professional Staff Congress, the faculty union, were assailed by state politicians, the press, and the chancellor and trustees of the CUNY system for allegedly anti-American statements. And in Canada, a professor at the University of British Columbia was vilified by federal and provincial politicians and the national and local press for critical remarks she made about US foreign policy at a conference of women's service organizations, and charged by the national police, the RCMP, with committing a hate crime.

This is just the beginning. It appears that we are at the start of a wholesale state-sponsored assault on civil liberties, if "anti-terrorist" legislation enacted in the United States and Canada is any indication. The squeeze on academic

---

1. See, for example, Ellen Schrecker's account of academia's response to the McCarthy period, in her *No Ivory Tower*.

freedom is just a small part of this process. But in this deepening crisis and its attendant security-conscious climate, the transparency of online instruction becomes not merely a matter of academic but of far larger political concern. Certainly administrators and political authorities will be in a position to monitor any and all such activities as never before, remotely and discreetly, without permission or acknowledgment, and they will have ready access to extensive electronic records of course content and communications.

Of course, we all believe we have nothing to hide, that what we or our students say online to one another is not only beyond reproach or suspicion but without any real significance. Why would anyone care about what goes on in my courses? But if the past is any guide, and it might well be, we should heed the hard-won lesson that in the end, in times such as these, guilt and suspicion are in the eye of the beholder.

October 29, 2001

Appendix

Business Goes Back to College[1]

There is nothing subtle about the way the academy reflects changing social conditions. At last spring's commencement exercises at the Massachusetts Institute of Technology, for example, Dr. Jerome Wiesner, then president of America's premier technical school, a former presidential science adviser in a quintessentially liberal administration, lauded a recent decision to deregulate oil and gas prices and decried the actions of "irresponsible regulators." The spirit of the times was even more aptly symbolized this commencement day by the fact that the president of a Houston-based consulting firm for the petrochemical industry (who is also president of the MIT Alumni Association) strode at the head of the faculty procession, wearing the Elizabethan parliamentary robes of the chief marshal and bearing the four-foot golden mace, symbol of academic authority. The ceremony captured the new reality of higher education in America: the ivory tower turned to plastic. For the third time in this century, the universities are undergoing a major transformation, in response to a fundamental shift in the economic and political climate. During the first decades of the century, the elitist liberal arts colleges were expanded and rapidly transformed into research and training centers for the then emergent electrical and chemical industries. In the 1940s the universities' primary ties were transferred from private industry to the federal government, as they became centers of contract research for military and other governmental agencies. The phase reached its full flowering in the policy think tank multiversity of the 1960s.

Now, the universities are shifting their allegiance back to the private sector and to the dominant power in that sector, the petrochemical industry under the goad of grave financial problems and in an effort to escape from governmental

---

1. This article, co-authored with Nancy E. Pfund, was published in *The Nation*, September 20, 1980.

red tape and scrutiny. The universities' new role will be to provide research and training in new industrial areas, particularly semiconductors, automation, and biotechnology, and bestow ideological sanction and scientific legitimacy upon Big Business's campaign against government "interference" in the economy. In the vanguard of this shift are large research institutions like Harvard, Stanford, MIT and the University of Michigan; leading the industry side are the major corporations in the petrochemical industry: Monsanto, Exxon, Dow, Du Pont and others. According to the annual survey of *The Chronicle of Higher Education*, universities have, in the last three years, received the largest increase in financial support from industry since 1920. The latest transformation, like those before it, is bound to have far-reaching consequences for the direction of research and technology, patterns of funding and appointments, the form and content of higher education, and the future of academic freedom.

The Industrial Connection

The industry campaign against government interference has gone through several phases during the past eight years, shifting from a simple negative campaign against government regulation to a more affirmative campaign for innovation or, most recently, reindustrialization, in which regulations are cast as obstacles to progress.

Industry's drive for closer collaboration with academia, for legitimization of its campaign, and for indirect state support of research and development neatly complements the needs of the universities. Falling enrollments, fiscal austerity, the overall decline in government support of research, as well as mounting resistance to federal demands for account and oversight of university affairs make the university eager for what Exxon's Edward David, Jr., has called the "industrial connection." The schools see it as a promising new source of funds and a respite from government scrutiny. Once the beneficiaries of the cozy collaboration with the government forged in the 1940s and 1950s, the universities now denounce government "interference." Thus, Charles Overberger of the University of Michigan complains about recent limitations on the peer review system, which in the past gave the universities control over government funding, challenges to indirect costing practices, restrictions on faculty salaries, growing emphasis on fiscal accountability, and the like. Wiesner of MIT argues that while the costs of research have increased, government support has declined; he also rails against what he calls "arbitrary political pressure on research," which, he claims jeopardizes long-

term projects, an important source of support for faculty and students, especially graduate students, and notes the drying up of discretionary funds and
the obsolescence of equipment and facilities.

In the controversy over Office of Management and Budget Circular A21,
which demanded greater fiscal accountability from universities, for example,
Wiesner protested vigorously that alleged attempts "to shackle [the universities]
to a detailed and rigid set of nationally administered rules and regulations . . .
swap progress for administrative convenience." He bemoaned "the erosion of
mutual confidence, the spirit of collaborative partnership with the government"
and decried what he called "despotic regulation," adding: "What we need and
what the country now needs is regulation of regulation." The OMB controversy reflects the ideological convergence of interest of industry, and the universities, and against the federal government. The upshot has been the industrial
connection, with academia groomed for the role of legitimator for industry.

Institutional Co-Optation

A bold statement of what this role entails can be found in a recently published
how-to book for people in management by Bruce Owen and Ronald Braeuti-
gam entitled *The Regulation Game*. Businessmen are told how to co-opt university based experts.

Regulatory policy is increasingly made with participation of experts, especially academics. A regulated firm or industry should be prepared whenever
possible to co-opt these experts. This is most effectively done by identifying
the leading experts in each relevant field and hiring them as consultants or
advisors, or giving them research grants and the like. This activity requires a
modicum of finesse; it must not be too blatant, for the experts themselves
must not recognize that they have lost their objectivity and freedom of action.

In their campaign against regulation, corporations have moved beyond
the crude tactics of co-optation of individuals to an institutionalized co-
optation on a grand scale. In their search for legitimization, they are buying into basic laboratory science, toxicology, epidemiology, and other areas
of public health, policy-oriented disciplines such as economics, political
science, and, of course, management science. The leased scholars in these
fields will provide the reams of data, the scientific publications, the cost
benefit analyses, the policy recommendations and, perhaps most important, the new generation of students lured by ample fellowships, new programs, and large research grants, bright and ambitious recruits who will

rarely think twice about the social and political implications of their fascinating scientific work.

Tied in with the scientific and policy oriented disciplines are the humanistic interdisciplinary programs established during the last ten years, thanks to the largesse of the Sloan (General Motors), Mellon (Gulf Oil), and Exxon Foundations. Under the aegis of such programs, philosophers and historians and social scientists will ponder the weighty theological questions associated with what *Fortune* called the "new religion" of cost benefit analysis and risk assessment. What do we mean by risk? How might societies and individuals best cope with risk? This new "discipline" will generate courses, journals, lectures, symposiums, and fellowships devoted to thinking about how much risk of respiratory disease, of cancer, of reproductive impairment, of pollution, or whatever can be quantitatively justified in the name of deregulation.

Exactly how this intellectual and scientific enterprise would be orchestrated is illustrated by the recent experiences of three elite universities, Harvard, MIT, and Stanford. Beginning roughly in the spring of 1978, during the height of the deregulation advertising campaign, Stanford and MIT each received requests from industry to begin discussions on the problems of risk and regulation. In November of that year, the provosts of the two institutions sent memorandums to selected faculty members soliciting comment. At MIT it was suggested that a faculty group be formed to explore "the problem of assessing and coping with risks resulting from scientific and technological innovation." This faculty workshop would ultimately hatch a "serious, long-term investigation, for which outside funding would be sought." At Stanford, the provost called for a conference on risk assessment and regulation and indicated that the initiative had come from B. F. Goodrich and an industry public relations firm.

At MIT, the initiative culminated in a new Harvard-MIT Joint Program on the Impact of Chemicals on Human Health and the Environment. The central thrust of the program was indicated in the report of a Harvard committee formed to consider the university's participation. "While strenuous efforts are being made and will continue to be made to prevent the further introduction of deleterious substances into the environment and, if possible, to eliminate those already present, one cannot believe that such efforts will ever be completely successful. Accordingly, there is now and will continue to be a need to deal in an ablative sense with the effects of exposure to one or another of these man-made environmental contaminants." In October 1979, the program was formally unveiled, bringing together health sciences, environmental sciences and engineering, policy analysis, especially regulatory policy, and the resources of the schools of law, government, management, medicine, public health, and arts and sciences.

The program's dominant themes faithfully reflected the industry campaign against regulation. "There is growing agreement among scholars," observed Chris DeMuth, a participant from Harvard, "that the process of adversarial regulation suffers from inherent shortcomings." These include, he said, "disregard of fundamental economic aspects of regulation and a well nigh universal suppression of innovation and competition, and protracted and unnecessary disputes between business and government over information disclosures, plant inspections, etc." Accordingly, he and his colleagues suggest, alternatives to regulation such as economic incentives for non-polluters should be explored. Funding sources for the Joint Program already include the Chemical Manufacturers Association, Dow, Monsanto, Exxon, and Du Pont, and MIT's Wiesner noted in his announcement that exploration is underway for further funding "at a level that will make such an ambitious program possible."

Objectifying Risk

At Stanford, the symposium idea centered on a similar notion of an "objective, unbiased examination of risk." As a university statement put it: "The current drive to reduce risk through government regulation is having and can have a severe negative impact on business, the economy and society, far out of proportion to the benefits society can expect to gain . . . Over-regulation, based upon emotion rather than sound science and logic, can soon become socially unacceptable . . . There is now a strong need for an objective examination of these issues." Here too the challenge is to depoliticize debates over risk and regulation by conjuring up an "objective" basis for decision making and in the process to defuse the political energies that gave rise to protective legislation in the first place. After toying with the symposium idea for a while, the Stanford administration and faculty decided that rather than merely talking about these problems, they would prefer to pursue some long-term projects with industry. Recently, preliminary negotiations with Goodrich and other firms took place, which planted the seeds of a collaborative philosophy.

The industrial connection has now won the official blessing of the National Academy of Sciences. In a recent address, the academy's president,

Philip Handler, who is currently under fire for alleged pro-industry bias and exercising undue influence on academy studies and reports, alluded to "substantial external pressures [that] seek to enlarge our role in educating the public to understand relative risks," among them "a consortium of chemically oriented companies [that] would like to encourage legislation that would call upon the academy to study and render judgments on risks of all types associated with chemicals utilized in industry." Exhorting his fellow scientists to condemn the "charlatans" and "naysayers" in their midst, i.e., those who sound the alarm on environmental and health hazards, Handler mentioned "another group of companies [that] has requested us to sponsor a meeting on the role of science in guiding public policy in regulating carcinogens." In accordance with these and similar requests, the academy has created a Committee on Risk and Decision Making, which is chaired by Howard Raiffa of the Harvard Business School and the Kennedy School of Government and includes among its membership several participants in the Harvard–MIT Joint Program.

Daedalus Takes a Flier

A final illustration of how the university is providing legitimization for the campaign against regulation, and of how industry is guiding the academic debates about risk, regulation, and innovation is provided by the history of a recent issue of *Daedalus*, the official journal of the prestigious American Academy of Arts and Sciences. In the spring of 1979, when the innovation phase of the industry campaign was just being launched, the editors of *Daedalus* got together with Exxon's Edward David, presidential science adviser under Richard Nixon and former chairman of the board of the American Association for the Advancement of Science. An apostle of progress through free enterprise, David supports deregulation, the reduction of "uncertainty" (tax, patent, antitrust, and regulatory policies), and economic incentives as a spur to innovation. A daylong conference was held at the Harvard faculty club for leading scholars in the fields of the history and sociology of technology and industry. Funding was provided by the Sloan Foundation. The conference was dominated by David and MIT provost Walter Rosenblith, originators of the Harvard-MIT program, and it was clear to at least some of the participants that they had an agenda, and it was not academic. The letter of invitation hinted at what it was about: "Is there a meaningful issue between those who argue that technology can and should be controlled by political decisions and those who believe it is best left to the disciplines of the marketplace or to its own imperatives? What is the role of government in directing technological development?"

On the face of it, these are, of course, entirely legitimate questions for the academic community to explore. But in this instance a close reading of the transcript of the proceedings reveals that the non-academic in the meeting, David, guided the discussion throughout. The deliberations, like those at most such academic gatherings, tended to be aimless, confused and boring, but whenever the discussion wandered, David would get the discussants back on the track: "There has to be some level of freedom in the development of technology, or else it will be so constrained that you will not get these great excursions that really provide the new versions." *Daedalus* editor Stephen Graubard did his part to keep matters in focus with statements such as: "I think some analysis of how the questions arise is in order, for example, the phenomenon of risk: how is risk being seen, why is risk defined in the way it is, by whom, issues of that sort. Ought we to be largely preoccupied with productivity, with technological innovation?" Then Harvard's Harvey Brooks came up with some particularly felicitous phraseology: "We have suddenly pushed very strongly for constraints on the development of technology because we have recognized the adverse effects of no constraints. Yet, we have tended to forget . . . that the inhibition of technological development can have just as many adverse secondary consequences as the promotion of technological development." When "regulation" is substituted for "constraints" and "industry" is substituted for "technological development," the meaning of all this jargonistic chatter becomes clear. "You know," David interrupted Brooks, "from the industrial side, I think you have put your finger on perhaps the critical issue that we see in industry today." The transcript, together with solicited papers on related topics, was published in the Winter 1980 issue of *Daedalus* (Volume 109, No. 1 of the *Proceedings of the American Academy of Arts and Sciences*). Not long thereafter, reprints of selected articles were distributed free to academics in the technology and society area, courtesy of the Bell Laboratories.

Reindustrializing Academia

Beyond their role as legitimator of the industry campaign against regulation, the universities are being called upon, and are avidly seeking to play, a role in innovation and reindustrialization programs. In this area, they play the dual role of lending academic sanction to industry's slogans and serving as the institutional conduit for taxpayer subsidies of industry in the areas of research and training.[2] As was the case with the military and the space programs, these new ventures are being justified in terms of national priorities and in the name of patriotism. But also, there's money in this latest hustle for fellowships, institutes, centers, research grants, and the like.

Although the relative decline in government support of university-based research has turned around slightly, with a 70 percent increase in Department of Defense funding in the last three years, the overall trend is toward greater infusions of money from private industry, stimulated by government incentives. Between 1955 and 1978, industrial support of academic research had dropped from 10 percent of overall support to less than 3 percent, according to R. E. Lyon of Exxon, while government support swelled. During this period, academic researchers chose to stay within the academy rather than go into industry, and industrial firms turned away from subsidizing university research in favor of research with the emphasis on practical application. Now the pendulum is swinging back the other way. Universities are seeking long-term research support, free of government overhead and red tape, and industrial firms are seeking greater control over the direction of new scientific and technological developments and a greater proprietary interest in these developments. The essential components of the industrial connection are government incentives for industry–university cooperation in research, such as tax breaks and more direct government seed money for joint ventures (for example, the National Science Foundation's "generic technology centers" and "innovation centers"); long-term contracts in basic and applied research (e.g., the Monsanto-Harvard and Exxon MIT contracts); cooperative research agreements, involving several firms and one or more universities, which allow for joint efforts without any clear violation of the antitrust laws (e.g., MIT's Polymer Processing Lab); reform of patent policy to foster uniformity from one contract to another and greater proprietary control over marketable

2. Harvard's much touted conference on productivity is a case in point. Held this past spring, the conference was cosponsored by Harvard, the New York Stock Exchange, and the US Senate Subcommittee on International Trade, and brought together academics, congressmen, and leaders from the corporate and banking communities (but no representatives from regulatory agencies, consumer or environmental groups, or labor). The most tangible product of the conference was a full-page advertisement in the *Wall Street Journal* (July 23, 1980) proclaiming that the United States "must strengthen its competitiveness" by, among other things, reducing the burdens of regulation and fostering innovation through government tax and other incentives. "The American people," the ad reads, "are aware of fundamental crisis in our economy and are ready to support extraordinary measures to reverse it."

research results; cross-fertilization between industry and university, including institutionalized consultant relationships, personnel exchanges, visiting faculty appointments, more elaborate industry oversight of research and teaching through advisory committees and the like, and more extensive contacts between students and faculty and industrial recruiters. All of these facets of the industrial connection are being promoted in the name of innovation, reindustrialization, and American industrial competitiveness.

Thus far, major areas of research include: industrial automation (e.g., Rensselaer Polytechnic Institute's work on computer interactive graphics with the International Business Machines Corporation, General Electric, Grumman, Lockheed, Prime Computer, and Bethlehem Steel; Carnegie-Mellon's collaboration with Westinghouse on a major NSF-funded robotics project; and Stanford's new Computer Aided Design/Computer Aided Manufacturing Center); integrated circuit design, especially for very large scale integrated systems at Cal Tech and MIT; materials structures and processing (e.g., Cornell's sub-micron structures lab, University of Delaware's composite materials project, and the Polymer Processing Lab at MIT, which now involves some two hundred corporations, including such giants as the International Telephone and Telegraph Corporation and General Motors).[3] The new MIT–Exxon "combustion" project is touted as a model for long-term cooperative research. Calling for the expenditure of $8 million over ten years, the contract is one of the largest and longest in duration of any university industry collaboration in research. MIT proposes the specific research projects from which Exxon selects the ones to be pursued, and Exxon gets an irrevocable, worldwide, nonexclusive, royalty-free license to any marketable results; MIT retains the patents. Exxon's David, who negotiated the contract, sees it as an important step toward long-term industry–university partnership and predicts that before too long industry will be underwriting 10 to 15 percent of university-based research.[4]

---

3. The deregulation campaign and the drive to automate are not unrelated. As the editor of Tooling and Production observed, "Surely we know that the best way to satisfy OSHA [Occupational Safety and Health Administration] and EPA [Environmental Protection Agency] regulations as they apply to the hazards and environment threatening workers is to design the worker out of the workplace."

4. It is worthy of note that during the push for the White House Domestic Policy Review effort, David worked closely with Frank Press of the Office of Science and Technology Policy on the administration's innovation initiatives; both were careful to restrict government support, and thus involvement, to basic research, so as to leave industry a free hand at the applied end of the research and development spectrum. Since then, however, and

Biotechnological Feedback

University–industry collaboration in automation and computer technology has been going on for decades. What we are seeing now is a new focus on "biotechnology." This latest growth industry is likened to the electronics explosion of the 1950s and 1960s and reflects, first, major new advances in recombinant DNA technology that render heretofore arcane laboratory techniques adaptable to large-scale production and, second, the move of the petrochemical firms, by means of merger, acquisition, and research, into the agricultural products and pharmaceutical fields that will make the most use of these new production processes. As *Chemical Week* put it in a headline recently, "DNA is on the way to chemicals." "The backdrop," explains Monsanto's Louis Fernandez, "is that many of our traditional businesses—plastics, fibers, and organic and bulk chemicals—will be growing at a rate substantially less in the next ten years than in the previous decade or two. We see greater potential for growth in the life sciences." Accordingly, Monsanto recently named Howard Schneiderman, dean of the School of Biological Sciences at the University of California at Irvine, to be its new senior vice president for research and development. Similar moves into the biological fields, and especially into the new microbiological world of recombinant DNA, have been made in recent years by Standard Oil of Indiana, Union Carbide, Standard Oil of California, Shell, and Occidental Petroleum.

By far the most ambitious bit of collaboration in the biomedical area thus far is Monsanto's $23 million cancer research project at the Harvard Medical School. More recently, the Harvard School of Public Health established an industrial associates program modeled on the industrial liaison program at MIT (and, indeed, set up by a former administrator of the MIT program) to keep fee-paying firms abreast of the latest developments in biotechnology and to foster individual and institutional consulting relationships and, possibly, more specific industry-sponsored research projects. In addition, Yale Medical School has established close ties with Miles Laboratory and, very recently, Stanford Medical School has stepped up plans for a new Institute of Biological and Clinical Investigation, which is essentially a biotechnology job shop. The architects of the institute "propose to develop a long-term continuous

---

somewhat to the dismay of the OSTP, Exxon has begun to argue against government involvement at the basic research end as well, pushing instead for more direct industry funding and control, as in the MIT combustion research project. This diversion of interest portends a conflict between the government science establishment science-based industry and merits close attention.

collaboration with the chemical, pharmaceutical, and engineering industries." "Collaboration with industry," they go on, "will be businesslike, with
contracts made by both parties involving commitment of the entire
Department of Medicine faculty." Calling their program "a model for industry–university collaboration," the promoters claim to "see few liabilities, if
any, in terms of academic freedom" and anticipate "no negative influence on
individual initiatives."

Besides the establishment of institutional collaboration, there has been a
rapid growth in the formation of new genetic engineering firms, reminiscent
of the state-university "spin-offs" of the electronics revolution. As with the
latter, companies created by research paid for with public funds are turned
into profit-making enterprises. Herbert Boyer of the University of California
at San Francisco started the new wave of entrepreneurialism when he founded Genentech in San Francisco in 1976, and he has been emulated by fellow
scientists at the University of Michigan, Harvard, and MIT who have rushed
to form new companies with names like Genex and Biogen. The stampede
was stimulated by several factors, not the least of which, of course, was the
advance in biotechnology itself. Other factors include relaxed regulations on
recombinant DNA work (even the controversial National Institutes of Health
guidelines do not as yet apply to private industry, although the hazards mul-
tiply with competitive commercial development); a flow of venture capital
into this new growth sector; federal support for research in bioengineering;
the support (and acquisition) by capital-rich petrochemical companies; and
the recent favorable Supreme Court decision on the patenting of living
organisms. The chief of Stanford's office of technology licensing, Neil Reimer,
has said he hopes that the institution's patents on recombinant DNA techniques "could be Stanford's Gatorade," an allusion to the economic success of
the drink spawned by researchers at the University of Florida.

Business on Campus

The third major transformation of American universities since the nineteenth
century is well under way, bringing the worlds of academia and industry closer by the hour. At Duke, Dartmouth, Cornell, Pace, Colorado, Northern Michigan, throughout the academic landscape, "executives in residence" are becoming a commonplace. Robert Lear, the former chairman of the Schaefer
Corporation, who is doing his residence at Columbia University, explains that
his "major effort is to get more business executives more interested and con-

cerned as to what is being taught and researched at the school . . . I'm a teacher . . . yet even in school I am still in business, still a part of the corporate scene." "The executives," Dean H. Jerome Zoffer, of the University of Pittsburgh, observes, "have an opportunity to plumb the contemporary student mind, and to participate in the training of their successors. And the students have an opportunity to see that executives are people like everyone else." They become "role models for the student body."

As the courts restrict the use of job tests, and academic credentials decrease in significance in rapidly changing areas of employment, industrial firms are getting more closely involved in the occupational guidance and training of college students. At the same time, notes Archie Lapointe of the National Manpower Institute, "education is fighting for its mission and is today a lot more receptive to cooperation with business and industry." Students are not the only focus of industrial attention. Larger firms, especially in the petrochemical industry, are beefing up their "university affairs departments" to promote good public relations with university faculty. Du Pont's academic ambassador spends a good deal of his time flying around the country to talk with established and up-and-coming academics, inviting them to give lectures, attend seminars, and otherwise become a part of the expanding corporate scene. Would-be critics are deliberately welcomed.

Finally, the increase in industry-sponsored scientific and technological research on campus in itself acts to orient students toward industry. As Herbert Fusfeld, director of the Center for Science and Technology Policy at New York University and past president of the Industrial Research Institute, editorialized in the July issue of *Science*, "Strong industry participation in mission oriented research institutes at universities and long-term projects between university research teams and single companies can provide opportunities for combining university research careers with economic growth of the private sector." No doubt, it will also provide jobs for graduates, consulting work for faculty, funds for facilities, fellowships and more, and this goes for all the other aspects of the industrial connection as well, but at what cost?

Academic Freedom for Sale

Universities in the United States have never been the autonomous, disinterested citadel of objective scholarship and social criticism that some lovers of learning imagine (although the persistence of this myth does tend to immunize these institutions from serious scrutiny and lend undue credibility to what is produced there in the name of science and scholarship). Nevertheless, the universities have provided a living for moderate dissenters, a vantage point from which to observe critically what is going on outside (if not inside), and a platform from which to address with relative safety controversial social questions. This role of the university as sanctuary should not be exaggerated but neither should it be dismissed. Perhaps the greatest danger posed by the renewed industrial connection is the very real threat to this relative independence at a time when we need to rethink fundamentally the central economic and political questions of modern industry and democracy. And there are other troubling thoughts as well.

It is not alarmist to wonder about the effects of industry's influence on the direction of scientific research. Once priorities have shifted from social need, the ostensible concern of government, to potential return on investment, which is business's main criterion, patents, proprietary interest, and secrecy will no doubt replace open debate, peer review, and publication as the norms of the academic scientific community. And it is of no little concern to responsible and respected researchers to contemplate the dilemmas of conflict of interest, censorship, and proprietary pressures once they have been thrown into this ethically murky world of dual alliance to science and to profit. And to believers in a truly competitive capitalism, as well as to the critics of corporate power, the industrial connection must seem yet another step in the direction of further consolidation of that power by the large corporations to the detriment of smaller businesses.

It is difficult to fathom corporate intentions and, of course, the motives of individual corporate officers will vary from executive to executive. How much of corporate America's involvement in university affairs is intentional or merely an accidental convergence of mutual interests is something we may never know. But the corporate–university relationship, whether developed by "accident" or deliberately, is a trend whose dangers should be explored.

There are some who might argue that the effects of industry funding of universities are no different from those of government funding. This is not correct for several reasons. The universities—the physical plant, equipment, staff, students, reputations, status—constitute a substantial social investment, one made over many years by generations of taxpayers, scholars, contractors, workers, scientists and the like. The universities, therefore, (and this includes those nominally private institutions that have thrived on public assistance since World War II) are an inherited resource that rightfully belongs to us all. This fact is recognized explicitly in the case of government support. Funds are given in the name of the citizenry by government to foster social ends that are shaped and defined in the political process by a multiplicity and diversity of ends, which oftentimes conflict. Access to this university resource can be demanded to insure that a plurality of interests are represented and, particularly, to include access for those without the means to purchase it, labor and consumers, for example. This is demonstrated in the recent suit brought by the California Rural Legal Association against the University of California charging that the university's research on harvesting machinery served only the interest of large growers at the expense of small growers and farm workers.[5]

Further, government support insures (except in the case of military research) public scrutiny over what is being done at public expense. Access and accountability are thus essential aspects of government support, and they can be fought for if denied. Because of the multiplicity of interests represented, government support also fosters a (relative) freedom of inquiry; there is no externally imposed "line" for the researcher to toe, no single master.

Falling in Line

With industrial support, however, the primary consideration guiding university funding is not social need but rather the profit needs of the firm itself. Moreover, the firm, in purchasing access to the university's resources, is blocking access to others and has no obligation to share that access (there is, after all, a finite number of buildings, personnel, laboratories). And the industry is getting far more than it is paying for: it is getting the cumulative social investment, one that took decades and sometimes centuries to create in return for little more than operating expenses. For example, Monsanto gave Harvard what appears to be quite a lot of money, $23 million. In return, they received access to the facilities of Harvard Medical School, a resource they could not have created with many times that amount. The firm has in essence transformed a part of a public sector social resource into a private sector preserve with little public scrutiny or accountability over its use of the facility.

Finally, with industrial support there is relatively less freedom for the researcher because there is now a single line to follow, the line of the generous

---

5. See Al Meyerhoff, "Agribusiness on Campus," *The Nation*, February 16, 1980.

benefactor. And this brings us back to the gravest concern of all, the future of academic freedom, the seeming depoliticization of discussion (in reality, the de-democratization of decision making), the stifling of debate. Already the debates over regulation have been transformed as a result of the industrial campaign in general and the industrial connection with universities in particular. Controversies over how best to regulate have given way to a severely polarized ideological conflict over whether or not to regulate at all. Since the issues are rarely articulated, there is little debate; rather, there is a tacit "lining up." Those who have continued to defend regulation in the interests of environmental protection and occupational health are now cast as radicals by those "in the know." As such, they are quickly isolated, placed beyond the pale of respectability (and promotion and funding), their names penciled off proposed projects and invitation lists to conferences and planning sessions, for fear they would cause trouble, rock the boat.

Effective censorship is rarely imposed from without, an unreflective and exaggerated habit of self-censorship, out of an unspoken fear of retribution, works much better. This is what has begun to take hold in the universities. As if by instinct, people are lining up "correctly," without instruction. Meanwhile, administrators intent on maintaining the lucrative industrial connection discipline, isolate, or eliminate those few who refuse to go along. The corporations need not say a word.

Index

commercial distance education, 5, 6–9,
11, 12–14
commercialization of academia, ix, 26,
28, 49, 93–94; in research, x, 37–38
Committee on Risk and Decision Making
(NAS), 104
commodification, 1–4, 6, 20, 27; of
instruction, 2, 28, 31–36, 49, 52, 93
computer-based instruction, 28, 29–30,
51. *See also* online education
Condren, Edward, 71, 81–82, 83
confidentiality clause, 42, 66
Congress, US, 59, 92
Connerly, Ward, 68, 71
Copyright Act of 1976, 43, 48, 66, 71,
80–81
copyright of course material, 6, 27, 55, 80,
81; instructor's right to, 71–75; protection of, 31, 37, 38–40, 49. *See also*
intellectual property rights
corporate consortium, 53
corporate funding, 27, 103
corporate partnerships, ix–x, 27, 88. *See
also* private sector and academia
corporate training, 29
corporatization of education, ix, x, 94
correspondence education movement,
1–24; Carnegie study of, 18–21; commercial firms, 5, 6–9, 11, 12–14; commodification of, 1–4; economics of,
7–9; Flexner's critique of, 16–18; modern partnerships compared to, 21–24;
university-based, 5, 9–21. *See also* distance education
Correspondence Education Research
Project, 20
cost benefit analysis, 102
course materials (courseware), 25, 27, 47,
52; instructors' rights to, 71–75, 91;
ownership of, 3, 32–33, 37, 38–40;
rights to, 22, 52. *See also* copyright;
intellectual property
criticism, xii
Crow, Michael, 22
Culpepper Foundation, 30
Cultech, 25

Daedalus (journal), 104–105
David, Edward, Jr., 100, 104, 105, 107
Davie, Kathleen, 55, 56
Defense Department, 87–90, 106
Democratic Party, 65
DeMuth, Chris, 103

deprofessionalization, 4, 85, 89–91
deregulation, 107. *See also* government
regulation
Dertouzos, Michael, 60
Digital Diploma Mills conference (1998),
56
digital diploma mills forum (1988), 54
digital divide, 92
distance education, 64, 92; commercial,
5, 6–9, 11, 12–14; military initiative
for, 87–90. *See also* correspondence;
online education
Distance Education and Training Council,
20
Distance Education Demonstration Program, 59
dropout money, 8, 11, 15
dropout rate, 58; in correspondence
schools, 7, 11, 12, 14, 15, 18, 23

E College, 86
education: automation of, ix, 33, 34, 90;
campus-based, 60–61; higher, 1–4, ix,
x, 20, 36, 94; just-in-
time, 89; quality, xii, 2, 4, 23, 34, 91, 92;
as social process, 54. *See also* distance
education; instruction; online education
educational commodities, 24
Educational Management Group, 31
education industry, 22, 29
educators, 4. *See also* faculty; instructors
Educom (Educause), 30, 33, 86
Edwards, Jeff, 58
Egbert, James, 12, 13, 17
elite and distance education, 92
enrollment, correspondence schools, 7,
11–12, 13, 14, 15, 17
extension programs, 39, 49. *See also*
UCLA Extension
Exxon (corporation), 102, 107, 108n

Face-to-face education, 35. *See also*
interpersonal relationships
faculty, x, 23, 29–30, 85, 110; academic
freedom of, 34, 90, 96; activism of,
53–54, 56–57, 61; and administration,
32, 34, 83; intellectual property rights
of, 37, 38–40, 43–46, 47–49, 55–56, 91;
labor issues of, 32–34; organizations
of, 55, 93–94; replaced by actors, 22;
role in correspondence education, 14,